Frontispiece:
"Mary in a dress of corn", painting by an unknown Frankish master,
1430.

The coloured illustrations:
"The adoration of the kings" by Stefan Lochner.

"Christ's Eve" — coloured lithograph serving as the basis for a puzzle,
around 1830.

Processions in honour of St. Martin in front of Neuss Cathedral — a
painting in the Impressionist style by H. Ritzenhofen, around 1910.

Josef Ruland

Christmas in Germany

Hohwacht 1992

CIP-Kurztitelaufnahme der Deutschen Bibliothek

Ruland, Josef:
Christmas in Germany / Josef Ruland. With contributions by Emil Barth . . .
[Transl. by Timothy Nevill]. — Bonn: Hohwacht, 1978.
Dt. Ausg. u. d. T.: Ruland, Josef: Weihnachten in Deutschland.
ISBN 3-87353-065-1

Translated by Timothy Nevill

© 2nd revised edition by Inter Nationes, Bonn 1992
Overall-Production: Druck Carl Weyler, Bonn
Printed in the Federal Republic of Germany

With contributions by

Emil Barth
Wolfgang Henrich
Johannes Keßler
Theodor Storm
Ulrich Tolksdorf

1

Contents

I.

Introduction

Christmas — no other celebration exerts such a far-reaching influence on all aspects of German life. Weeks, and even months, beforehand, entire branches of industry and commerce start to prepare for this time of year. It is as if public life in all its manifestations is moving towards these holy days. Since that is the case, everyone in our country is affected. No-one can escape the influence of this great festival. It is a celebration for everyone. Anyone who wants to get to know the Germans properly should therefore spend Christmas in Germany. The festival of Christmas is celebrated all over the world but nowhere else is this celebration so rich and profound as in Germany. It has survived all kinds of political developments. Attempts to change or do away with Christmas have failed miserably.

This little book is meant to serve as an introduction to Christmas in Germany with its colourful and remarkable customs and practices. It provides a sober description of reality rather than enthusiastic extollation. Of the latter there is more than enough with over a hundred new works about Christmas presented year after year at the Frankfurt Book Fair at the end of September. That fact alone shows how important Christmas is in this country.

None of the diverse nuances and aspects of this splendid and noble time of year are left out of account here. Attention is devoted to regional characteristics, which still flourish despite radio and television, so far as they seem necessary to this "stock-taking". Historical influences and derivations are presented to the extent that they still exert an influence today in this or that custom and even entire complexes of usages. And they do exert a greater impact than we are ready to concede at first sight. The publisher and the author place great value on a detailed list of contents, organised chronologically and in terms of groups of customs, and hope that serves as a substitute for an alphabetical index. The list of contents should help the reader to find his way quickly.

Finally we wish the reader as much pleasure in "Christmas in Germany" as we had in preparation of the book. If our descriptions tempt, then come and spend Christmas in Germany! We wish you:

A Merry Christmas!

This drawing comes from a "Golden Christmas Book" dating from 1878. It was intended to show readers how a "completely decorated Christmas Tree" should appear.

II.

The first Bringers of Gifts before Christmas

Every year, when the leaves turn brown and golden and start falling, when the evenings are drawing in and the grapes are gathered along the Moselle and Rhine, children begin to get excited. St. Martin's Day (November the 11th) is no longer far off — and that is their festivity. This festivity is just for children. Many look forward to it throughout the year. Their parents too since there is no finer children's celebration than Martin's Eve with merry-making in villages and smaller towns on November the 10th.

School-children throughout the north-west of the Federal Republic (especially in Westphalia and in the areas surrounding the rivers Rhine, Ruhr, Moselle, Lahn, Nahe, and Main) take part in extensive processions after dark. They carry Chinese lanterns and home-made lights, torches, and hollowed-out turnips as was the custom in earlier times. Highly artistic housings are devised for these lamps. A multiplicity of motifs and figures are then cut out of the strong cardboard from which these cylinders, balloons, stars, and rhombus forms are constructed. Colourful transparent paper is stuck over the cut-out designs so that a tranquil light is diffused when the candle inside the lantern is lit. On such an evening lights in a multitude of colours are transported through the streets, often on long poles.

Processions by night

School classes and teachers take great pride in creating extremely original lamps providing great light. These are often minor works of art with a great diversity of motif and material. Both religious and secular themes are popular, wood-cut-like depictions of scenes from the life of St. Martin, and animals and plants. Everyone enjoys the sight of these processions making their way through the streets, accompanied by groups of musicians.

Singing children follow these bands. Their favourite song tells of St. Martin, the Roman soldier who rode one cold day through the countryside and met a beggar asking for alms. As a soldier

Martin had neither money nor anything else he could give the poor man. Then he thought of the warm cloak he was wearing. Without delay he took off the cloak, cut it in two with his short sword, and gave one half to the beggar crouching at the road-side. According to legend, Christ appeared to him in a dream the following night, saying: "Martinus, who is not yet baptised, protected me against the cold".

The Saint's life   That was a sign — continues the legend — that the heathen soldier would soon be baptised, and from that time onwards devote himself totally to the service of God and the Church. In the year 372 A. D. Martin was appointed Bishop of Tours, which was still under Roman rule. He was celebrated for his piety and humility, and died in high esteem.

When the Franks succeeded the Romans as rulers of Gaul a hundred years later, they viewed this holy man as their national saint and honoured him greatly. The Saint's cloak, the cappa, was among the most revered of the surviving relics. Capella, the diminutive of cappa, also became the word used to designate the little church in which the relic was safeguarded, and the word chapel derives from that. The chapel in Aachen's imperial palace, one of the main centres for veneration of the Saint, became a model for the whole of Europe. Many churches were dedicated to St. Martin and named after him. Veneration of St. Martin accompanied the Franks wherever they extended their empire, whether to the west or the east. St. Martin's Day is therefore a very special day right up to the present throughout western and south-western areas of Germany, and also in districts the other side of Germany's western frontiers. Even today many older people follow the Middle Ages in experiencing St. Martin's Day as the start of the dark and cheerless transition from autumn to winter.

The Martinmas fire   That is why this day has, from time immemorial, involved a celebration of light and of fire, and been marked by great lamplight processions and the burning of huge piles of wood out on the fields. The processions customary in the Rhineland, Westphalia, and parts of Central Germany have already been mentioned. The custom of the Martinmas fire is older and was initially more widespread. Weeks before St. Martin's Day, combustible material is collected by school-children in the villages of the Eifel, Westerwald, Hunsrück, Taunus, Rheingau, and Sauerland. Old baskets, wood shavings, cardboard boxes, branches, straw, old beams, and even car tyres are scrounged and piled up. These fires, sited in high places where they can be seen for long distances, are then lit at ceremonies on St. Martin's Eve.

St. Martin and his church at Oberwesel. Wall painting from around 1520.

Rail travellers from Mainz to Düsseldorf in the late afternoon of November the 10th can see these fires blazing away on the hills on either side of the Rhine. A chain of fire runs along the Rhine valley, and only comes to an end where the hills leave the river and the cities start. People there fear that such fires might spread to the houses so children have to be content with processions.

As already indicated, such fires were more important than torch-light processions until far into our century. It used to be said that the fields would be fertile and survive the winter for as far as the fires were to be seen. The ashes were also scattered across the countryside. In some places, parents exhorted their children to pray as they circled around these fires. There are many Martin's mountains, hills, or rocks, named after the fires lit there every year.

Torchlight processions were introduced much later. In the Rhine-land, Düsseldorf claims the honour of having been the first larger town to have inaugurated such a procession. The first such event at Bonn was as late as 1920. The focus of the procession is the mounted figure of St. Martin as a Roman soldier. The horse should be white so as to accord with an old song about the Saint. Seeing the knight riding along in his Roman armour of chain-mail, golden helmet, and red cloak is an impressive sight for children. After the procession has come to a stop, the Martin takes up position in an open space and the children march past once again. There is a final loud drum-roll, and the trumpets and flutes, the pipes and bells, resound for the last time this year.

Years ago, the city of Düsseldorf devised a special attraction for bringing the procession to an end. When it reaches the former princely residence and the large equestrian statue in the old part of the town, the children gather around the four sides of the courtyard. The St. Martin then re-enacts the division of the red cloak with his sharp sword and hands one half to a beggar kneeling before him on the ground. The children sing a song describing what is happening: "St. Martin shares his warm cloak, divided with a single stroke".

Gifts on St. Martin's Day Other West German towns have followed suit. In 1977 Bonn staged this scene on its historic market-place for the first time in the hope that such an impressive spectacle would promote charity in young people. Some places present all the younger children with a bun on St. Martin's Day itself. This can be a simple currant bun, or it can be a bun shaped like a person, animal, plant, ring, horse-shoe, etc, etc. In the latter case, it is usually between 20 and 30 cm in length with a head, two currants as

St. Martin's Eve at Düsseldorf — the title page of "L'Univers Illustré", a Paris magazine (11. 11. 1865).

eyes, a body, and two legs. This is made of high-quality leavened dough, and is exceptionally popular among children.

From house
to house
The day is not yet over though. After the fire has died down and all the children have trouped past St. Martin, they split up into small groups and go singing through the locality. In their song they ask at houses and shops for a little gift. "Hier wohnt ein reicher Mann, der uns was geben kann". A rich man lives here and can give us something — according to almost all the Rhenish versions of this song, despite local variants in text and tune. The children sing out since the louder they sing, the more they may get. Ten, twenty, possibly even more groups of children hurry from house to house, and are usually given biscuits, sweets, apples, nuts, and sometimes even money.

Elsewhere in the Federal Republic of Germany the customs surrounding St. Martin's Eve are different. After the Reformation, there was no more singing to St. Martin in Protestant areas since veneration of saints had been abolished. Children knew how to look after their interests though. In order to save their celebration, they sang their songs in honour of Martin Luther, who had, after all, been born on November the 10th. Such a version of the Martin's song is mainly found in the Protestant parts of Westphalia and Central Germany (particularly around Erfurt), and also in the coastal towns of Northern Germany. Where not even that was tolerated, there arose songs without any reference to the name of Martin. They all have in common some reference to light. One song starts "Lantern, Lantern, Sun, Moon, and Stars", and another begins "I go with my lantern".

Both Church and secular authorities tried to ban such pursuits but young people have stood by their right to go from house to house, seeking gifts, on specific days. A remarkable tradition persists right up to the present day around Arnstadt in Thuringia. What is known as the "dancing bear" makes its way through the village one day in November. This is a man cased in straw, led on a chain by a "keeper". Exotically costumed schoolchildren follow after this couple. The company stops in its tracks and the children sing a song wherever there is a cross-roads, a large farm, or anything promising. The bear has to keep dancing as long as the song continues. When it is over, the children get apples, pears, biscuits, nuts, and even bacon. The procession then moves on again. At every stop the bear and its keeper get a schnapps, and after a time the effect of the alcohol becomes apparent. When the procession has come to an end, the children go into the pub to share around all they have collected whilst the bear and its keeper trot home to sleep themselves sober.

This impressive image of St. Martin was rediscovered in 1935 at the little village of Bassenheim near Koblenz. It is thought to date from 1239 and to be the work of the creator of the celebrated figures at Naumburg Minster.

Heathen forerunners

St. Martin's Day is also celebrated in Southern Germany — but not as a time for torchlight processions and fires. The "Furry Man", a noisy disguised figure ringing bells, rattling chains, and cracking whips appears on Martin's Eve between the Main and the Danube, and around Nuremberg, Erlangen, Ulm, and Nördlingen.

In the Bohemian and Bavarian Forests, St. Martin's Day is herdsman's day. In earlier times, herdsmen terminated their agreements with local communities or owners of large numbers of animals on this day in order to establish new conditions of service. They also "drove out the wolf" with much noise and turmoil. Legend reports that modesty drove the man who was to become the patron saint of herdsmen into a goose-pen when he heard he was to become a Bishop. The Martinmas goose is well-known all over Germany, even where — as in the Erzgebirge — nothing else remains of such traditions. Silesia, Pomerania, and East Prussia seem never to have celebrated St. Martin's Day. The age and influence of the Franks had long passed when they were Christianised. There are, of course, exceptions even there. Former inhabitants of Ratibor in Upper Silesia report, for instance, that there used to be a lantern procession in November with groups of people going through the town singing "religious" songs.

Everyone knew though about the custom whereby domestic servants either changed their job or extended an existing agreement on this day. When reforms abolishing serfdom were introduced in Prussia in 1806/7, the authorities chose the 11th of November for this purpose.

Only where the office of herdsman was of great importance were the staffs of office returned to the feudal lord on St. Martin's Day. That mainly happened in the Harz Mountains and in Bavaria. Cattle went into their stalls for the winter on St. Martin's Day, and the staffs were used again when the animals returned to their pastures in the spring. The first snow usually fell around the beginning of November, brought from heaven by the Saint's white horse.

Martin the proud horseman

Heathen, Pre-Christian, and Christian elements have therefore been preserved up to the present day. Analysis of surviving traditions and customs shows that Christian elements have been superimposed on earlier ways of celebrating this day. The Church skilfully put the emphasis on the revered Bishop as Christianity was generally accepted. The proud horseman, who shared his cloak with a beggar out of love for his fellow creatures, was a symbolic figure according with the taste of princes and peoples. That is why many scholars see this type of Christian knight in the equestrian statues at such great cathedrals as Bamberg and Magdeburg. The most vivid depiction of this kind was discovered between the two world wars at the church in a small village near Koblenz. This Bassenheim horseman must have been created by a master — perhaps the man who carved the figures at Naumburg cathedral. The rider has already gone past the beggar when he cuts his cloak in two, and leans back to drop one half into the latter's raised hands.

III.

St. Nicholas and Ruprecht

Martin's Eve and its procession have not long passed when children in Germany set about preparing for another pre-Christmas festivity. This is the festival of St. Nicholas. "No other saint is so universally and so joyously celebrated" — writes the authoress of a celebrated book on Nicholas. Santa Claus (as he is called in the Anglo-American sphere) is celebrated everywhere — in England and the Netherlands, in North America and in South Africa. He is among the bringers of gifts and presents, and there are still parts of Germany where it is St. Nicholas — rather than the Christ Child — who brings presents for "good" children.

St. Nicholas' Day

Such reverence has long existed. In the year 1087, some devout Italian seamen made off to Bari in Southern Italy with the bones of the saint from Myra in Asia Minor, where he had served as a Bishop and died. Within 80 years a place of commemoration had been established at Metz in Lorraine. From there veneration of the saint spread down the Rhine into Germany, to the Low Countries, and to England. Of no other saint are so many miracles reported. He is said to have performed some of these miracles at sea or in harbour, and thus became patron saint of sailors. Wherever these mariners came, they had a church or chapel built in honour of their saint. In all the towns along the Rhine, there are statues of St. Nicholas and churches are often dedicated to him. The Hanseatic League took reverence for St. Nicholas to the Scandinavian countries. Königsberg, Elbing, and Danzig had churches dedicated to the saint as a matter of course. St. Nicholas's church close to Hamburg harbour still welcomes mariners from all over the world.

Veneration of St. Nicholas

Nicholas also became the patron saint of an even larger group of people — of students at local schools and universities throughout Europe. The saint is said to have brought back to life three children who had been murdered and stored as pickled meat in vats in the house of a bloodthirsty butcher. That is why a tub in

Nicholas, patron saint of students

which three children are sitting is frequently depicted at the holy Bishop's feet. Even before veneration of St. Nicholas was instituted, these children received presents on the 6th of December. Throughout the year they had carried out their duties as choirboys and ministrants at church festivals, and now received a small reward — such as money, apples, nuts, and honeyed confectionary — from the hands of the faithful. And who was better suited to bear these gifts than the saint who had become the children's patron? It was not long before this custom applied to all children and then adults too, and people started to give one another presents on this day.

The children's saint

From an early date, a person representing the saint handed these gifts out to children. An adult used to — and still does — put on a Bishop's robe, and also has a Bishop's mitre and staff. He then goes to the houses where children live, and takes the presents out of the big sack carried around by his attendants. The children sit and pray and sing until the sound of a bell announces that the Saint is entering their house. In early times, children chose a child Bishop from their midst on December the 5th, the evening before the festival, and this representative performed the allotted tasks for two days. In large families nowadays, a relative, friend, or even the father dresses up as a Bishop and examines the children. "Have you been good? Have you prayed diligently? Have you been well-behaved towards your parents and teachers?" This custom is very old. Abraham a Santa Clara, the celebrated Augustinian court preacher at Vienna towards the end of the 17th century, has described what was involved. "It is a very old custom that Nicholas should put something in children's shoes today. He comes on the previous evening though to examine whether the children have been well instructed by their teacher, tutor, schoolmaster, arithmetician, grammarian, and other pedagogues in matters of faith, spelling, syntax, reading and writing, computation, and languages. The Nicholas thus asks how children have behaved throughout the year? Whether they pray gladly? Whether they are obedient to their parents and teachers? Whether Hans and Paul are perhaps too lazy? . . ."

Little has changed there up to the present day. Such a distribution of presents takes place everywhere, even where people no longer believe in Saints and their miraculous powers.

The Saint's attendant — Ruprecht

The Saint does not come alone though. To the children's dismay, he is attended by a black figure wrapped up in old clothes, sacking, or furs. This figure has different names all over Germany. In Southern Germany it is known as the Krampus, in North-West Germany as Pelzebock or Pelznickel, in the Rhineland as Hans Muff, and in Silesia as Bartel or the Wild Bear. In Hesse there are

St. Nicholas — a Speculatius mould from Kevelaer on the Lower Rhine,
dating from the end of the 18th century.

St. Nicholas and his attendant Ruprecht, around 1820.

two figures, Gumphinkel and the Bear, and in the Palatinate either Nicholas or his attendant is known as Stappklos, the plodder and grumbler. Close to the Dutch border and in the Netherlands this attendant is called Black Pit. In middle-class families though, the most celebrated name since the Reformation has been Knecht Ruprecht.

This black man carries on his back the sack containing all the delights to come. He also carries the rod which the holy man

St. Nicholas with his rod. Drawing by Ludwig Richter (1855) whose romanticising illustrations have remained popular up to the present-day.

seems to need. Disobedient children are punished with the rod. At the same time, Ruprecht growls, rattles his chains, or shows the teeth in his black face so that it is not just children who are scared of him. "Just wait until Ruprecht comes" is still a threat in many German families.

That was also the reason why people in some areas forego a personal visit from St. Nicholas. In these places he brings the presents secretly by night. Children put out their shoes on the

Ruprecht. Engraving by Golz, 1784.

previous evening so that the Saint can put something in. In earlier times when people still had an open fireplace in their home, children put their shoes under the chimney. Today they put them under the bed or next to a radiator. It is still said though that sometimes — even in our modern world — there is a little rod in some shoes as a warning for the recipient.

In Silesia the holy man came down to earth on a golden cord from heaven so as to visit the sleeping children. On the North Sea, Nicholas comes by ship. Even around Bad Tölz in Bavaria, children here and there put out paper ships as receptacles for gifts. It is not without good reason that Nicholas is the patron saint of those who go to sea. In most areas though, the Saint comes riding through the sky on either a donkey or a white horse. The animal has long distances to cover so a little bundle of hay is laid out for it alongside the child's plate or shoe. A children's song for Nicholas' Day tells the Saint to put his donkey under the table where hay and oats are waiting.

That involves a level of tradition extending back into pre-Christian times before the Saint existed. The Gods still ruled then, and, according to Germanic mythology, stormed with their horses across the sky on autumn and winter evenings. Further mention of this will be necessary.

With the Reformation, St. Nicholas was increasingly transformed into an old man, perhaps a hermit or a kind of mountain spirit, who over the centuries was given the name of Santa Claus. He is the friendly old man with the long white beard, the fur-trimmed hood and the capacious warm coat, who comes down to earth on a sledge out of the sky as if in a snow-storm in order to distribute presents. As late as 1778, the authorities in Hesse forbade the custom of having a Nicholas, dressed up as a Bishop, going the rounds. The transition to Santa Claus helped preserve children's pleasure and avoided infringement of a traditional practice. This name is preserved in some Protestant areas up to the present day. The people of the Altmark around the Lower Elbe in North Germany give the name of Klaasbuur or Burklaas to the person who make his way through the villages from early to mid-December. In Bremen, Nicholas is celebrated with singing. Small groups of children, whose costumes are reminiscent of those of the Three Wise Kings, go from house to house, singing of Good Nicholas knocking at all doors. They accompany this with rhythmic beating of the earth so as to emphasise both the song and their request for presents. Other names are given to the Nicholas figure in Mecklenburg (Rauklas), Schleswig-Holstein (Bullerklaas), and in Friesland (Sünner- or Sunnerklas) where he wanders from farm to farm.

St. Nicholas –
Santa Claus

The further East you go though, the fewer the links with the Christian Saint. The Pomeranians have their Ashman, the West Prussians their Shaggy Goat, and the East Prussians of the plains their Rider or their Bag o' Bones Goat, which became the Yule Goat around the Baltic. Animal skins and straw are among the attributes of these figures. They no longer accompany a man who

Somewhat sinister – and not just for children: the "Buttenmänner" (also known as "Straw Men") who accompany St. Nicholas in the area around Berchtesgaden. (Wolf Lücking)

brings gifts. They are independent, and, above all, they demand presents for themselves.

After the war, a number of East Prussian farmers were settled on a former military training area in the Eifel. They were given land, and they established communities. After a number of years they had established roots and started to feel at home in the area, and it was then that they took up a traditional custom once again. This involves a young man receiving a white hobby-horse which he then "rides" from house to house. He is accompanied by other figures such as a chimney-sweep, a Santa Claus with attendant, and another young man carrying a life-size doll on his back.

Researchers concluded that this was a case of maintenance of pre-Christian customs. Figures that cannot be of Christian origin have also been preserved in Nicholas Day traditions even in the Alemannian and Bavarian South of Germany. These include such untranslatable figures as Klause and Zantichloise, Nicolo and Butz, Rumpelklas and Klaubauf. They are usually young fellows who dress as if for Carnival. With blacked faces and terrifying masks adorned with cows' horns, they rush, dance, or dawdle through the villages. Housewives gladly give them something so as to get these scary figures away from their frightened children as quickly as possible. Close to the Czech frontier in the Bavarian Forest, around Regensburg, and in the Inn-Region, particularly remarkable figures have survived as the Niglo, the Budl-frau, and the Butzenbercht, involving associations with fertility and the revival of life in the coming year. Niglo is viewed from an early age onwards as being the patron of girls who want to marry, and popular superstition in the more remote corners of the Alps still sees him as the bringer of children into the world. It is Niglo — and not the stork, the spirit of the fountain, or a blossoming tree — that provides a little brother or sister. Experts also interpret the rod that Ruprecht wields so threateningly as a life-engendering magic wand rather than an instrument of punishment.

Pre-Christian origins

Anyone who travels through Germany in early December in the hope of encountering Nicholas will meet with many figures that are vaguely reminiscent of the holy Bishop but are often anything but children's friends. It is not therefore surprising that in the big cities the influence of liberal circles, of other countries, of television, and not least of the large department stores has transformed the Holy Man (as he is called in the Rhineland) into Father Christmas. The latter has now taken over the role of bringer of presents. In some families and in some places he still distributes his gifts on December the 5th but he increasingly takes the place of the two original bringers of gifts in a child's heaven — Nicholas and the Christ Child. In Heinrich Hoffmann's "Struwwelpeter", the great Nicholas may still duck bad boys in the giant ink-pot but his dress and appearance reveal that he has already become Father Christmas.

Nicholas today

"Nicholas became angry and full of rage/as you can see on this very page". Dr. Heinrich Hoffmann, the creator of the famous "Struwwelpeter", made the most of Nicholas in the bringing up of children.

IV.

Christmas Markets

On the 25th of December 1772, Johann Wolfgang von Goethe wrote a letter (that has since become celebrated) from his home town of Frankfurt am Main to his friend Johann Christian Kestner. "Early on Christmas Day. It is still night, dear Kestner. I rose so as to be able to write again by candlelight in the morning, which brings back pleasant memories of earlier times. I had coffee made for myself in honour of this festive day, and want to write to you until day breaks. The watchman has already played his tune from the tower. I woke up to that. . . As I went across the market and saw the many lights and toys, I thought of you . . ." *Christmas Markets*

The market Goethe referred to was the Christmas or the Christ Child's market, also known in places like Stuttgart as the Christmas Fair. The most famous German Christmas market is at Nuremberg. From the beginning of Advent, booths and stalls are set up on the market-place where you can buy everything you need for Christmas: decorations for the tree and candles, crib figures and Nuremberg's celebrated gingerbread (which is mainly baked and consumed at Christmas), Christmas trees, and presents for Christmas Eve. As early as 1697 a citizen of Nuremberg wrote: "Some days before the festival when the Protestant Churches devoutly celebrate the incarnation of Christ the Lord, a market is held here that is usually called the 'Child's Market' or, more fully, the 'Christ Child's Market'. Almost the entire market place is covered with wooden stalls . . . where all kinds of goods . . . are set out for sale". The writer adds that small children believe the Christ Child buys its wares there. That is so even today. Fathers and mothers who go with their children to this market still say: This is where the Christ Child comes.

In Munich the market is also called the Christ Child Market, and is set up on the Marienplatz in front of the Town Hall. The people of Munich say that their market dates back for over 600 years, and was mentioned as early as 1310. Be that as it may, one of Munich's citizens recently wrote of the Christ Child Market that

"Frankfurt Christmas Market" on the Römerberg. Drawing from Dr. Heinrich Hoffmann's "King Nutcracker and poor Reinhold".

"When in the early dusk the lights of the tall Christmas tree shine out and groups of people from the mountains sing the pious old shepherd's and crib songs, there develops an atmosphere akin to a religious service".

Many other German towns and cities have adopted such a market. Berlin and Hamburg took this step as early as the 18th century. Such a market attracts many people, strolling past the stalls and displays to see what's new and all the fine things on show. Freiburg im Breisgau held its first Christmas market in 1972, and this is not solely devoted to Christmas trees and decorations. Artists and craftsmen see such markets as the right place for exhibiting and selling their goods — baskets and woodcuts, shoes and pottery.

Walking through such a market really is an exceptional experience. Children enjoy this most of all. The smells of fir resin and roasted almonds intermingle. Then there are all the lights from the stalls and the little stoves where sausages are fried and chestnuts roasted. Songs and the sounds of music fill the air. The closer it gets to Christmas, the colder it usually becomes. If snow falls, a hushed mood prevails at these markets. Tranquillity takes over from all the busy activity. There are many people who come from far away in the world outside to spend just a few days in the Federal Republic over Christmas. Despite the limited time at their disposal, a visit to such a Christmas market is a must for them.

Christmas today on the Römerberg in Frankfurt am Main.

There is a rather pleasing story from Frankfurt. Dr. Heinrich Hoff-   ***Struwwelpeter***
mann, the medical practitioner previously mentioned, lived there
in the 1840s. His daughter Lina was born in the city on December
the 11th, 1844. Mother and daughter needed to rest so Hoffmann
himself set about finding presents for his children. He did not
find the right thing though — even at the Christmas market. His
son Carl wanted to have a picture book so he had no alternative
but to make such a book himself. It was ready on Christmas Eve.
A year later Dr. Hoffmann had it printed. Within 30 years it had
gone through 100 editions. This book became famous all over
the world as "Struwwelpeter".

Christmas markets were unknown along the Rhine until recently.
The Bonn market has been in existence for less than twenty
years. All the same, it has gained so many friends within this short
time that no-one would like to be without it now.

Toy stall from a Christ Child Market in the early 19th century.

V.

Letters to Santa Claus and Christmas Money

A list of wishes is almost indispensable for the distribution of gifts at Christmas. When parents, grand-parents, other relations, or friends want to give their children, grand-children, nieces, nephews, etc, something for Christmas, they often ask: Have you made a list? When the signal has been given, children, small and big, set about drawing up a list, often illustrated with drawings. "Dear Christ Child", or "Dear Father Christmas" — runs such a letter. "I should like to have . . ." — and then there follows a list of all that the child wants for Christmas: clothes, toys, books, cookies, sports gear, and all kinds of request, some of which can be satisfied, some not. Which wishes are fulfilled depends on bringers of gifts, their financial situation, and their attitude to what is involved. The clever mother or father will head off wishes entailing unfulfillable expectations:

Lists of wishes

Incomes have risen in the Federal Republic in recent decades though, and these lists sometimes include pretty expensive wishes. Bicycles and cameras, mini-computers, CD players, musical instruments, elaborate construction kits, tin soldiers, school requisites, shoes, suits, and dresses are asked for even in less well-off homes. There is no better index of general social attitudes, and there are few parents who are not ready to spend their last Pfennig on fulfilling their children's wishes.

The Christmas bonus

When you consider that entire branches of industry live from the Christmas trade, it is understandable that the big department stores fill their windows and catalogues with everything the market offers. Money is borrowed, debts are incurred, and exchanges are arranged so as to make sure of sharing in these many possibilities.

Faced with this situation, employers and trade unions negotiated a financial bonus for Christmas so as to prevent employees getting involved in expenditure exceeding their normal budget. The Christmas bonus, usually an additional (i.e. thirteenth) monthly

4411 CHRISTKINDL
5
25.11.1977

CHRISTKINDL

Special post-mark from the "Christ Child" post office and "Lists of Christmas wishes" from the fifties and sixties.

Liebes
Ich wünsch
ein Paar Ro
ein Ministeck
ein Puzzlespiel.
ein Tafelschoner.
eine Märchenplatte
ein Sandmännchen

Wunschzettel von Heinrich...
Ich wünsche mir am Christkindl
Ein Paar lange Strümpf
Ein Paar Lederstiefel
Eine Zimmerlampe
Ein Paar Zopfspangen
Eine Garnitur Unterwäsche
einen bunten Teller
eine schöne Puppe
einen schönen Weihnachtsbaum

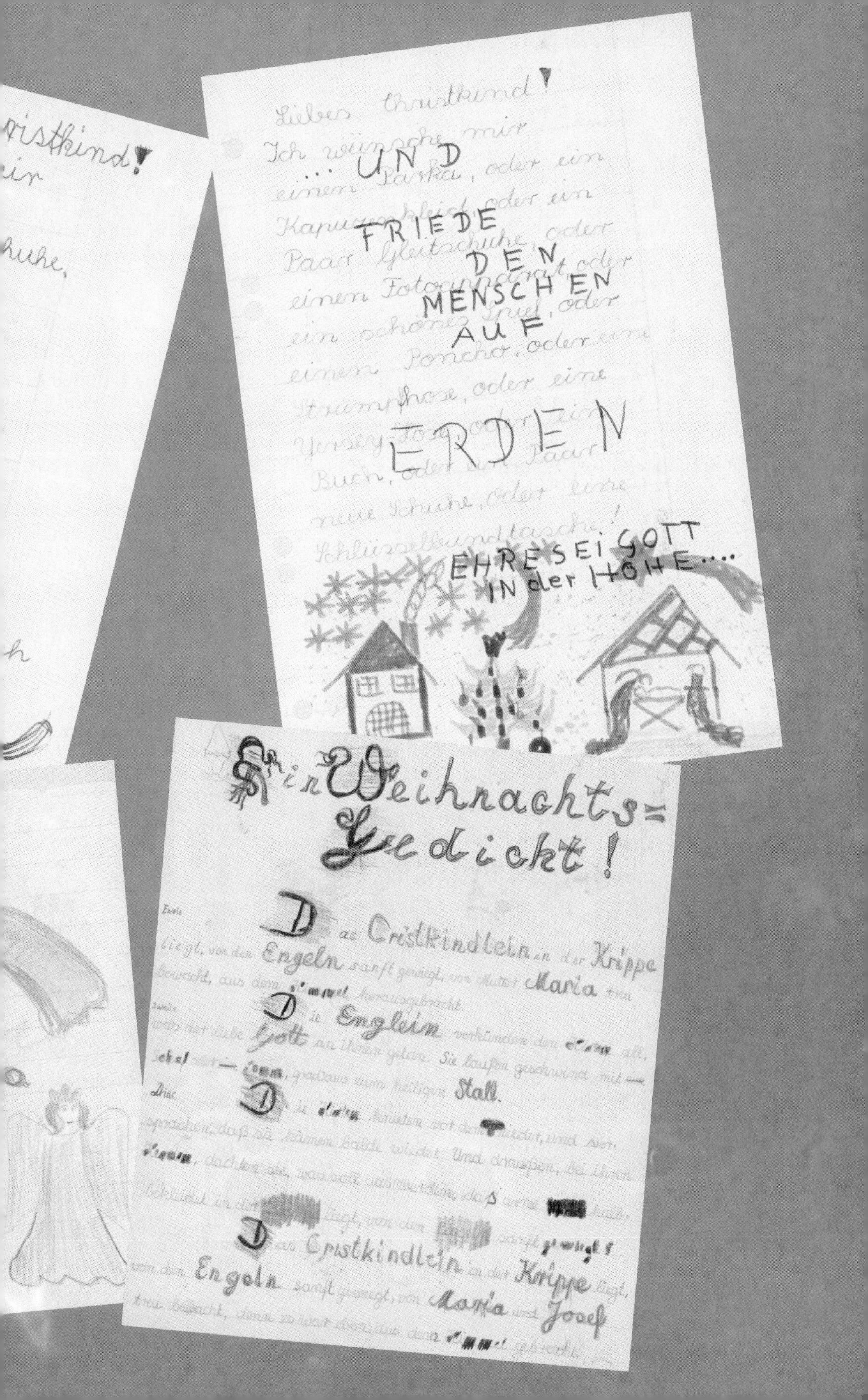

Liebes Christkind!
Ich wünsche mir
einen Parka, oder ein
Kapuzenkleid, oder ein
Paar Gleitschuhe, oder
einen Fotoapparat, oder
ein schönes Spiel, oder
einen Poncho, oder eine
Strumpfhose, oder eine
Jersey-Jacke, oder ein
Buch, oder ein Paar
neue Schuhe, oder eine
Schlüsselbundtasche!

... UND FRIEDE DEN MENSCHEN AUF ERDEN

EHRE SEI GOTT IN der HÖHE ....

...Christkind!
...ir

...huhe,

...h

Ein Weihnachts=Gedicht!

Erste
Das Christkindlein in der Krippe
liegt, von den **Engeln** sanft gewiegt, von Mutter **Maria** treu
bewacht, aus dem Himmel herausgebracht.

Zweite
Die **Englein** verkünden den Menschen all,
was der liebe **Gott** an ihnen getan. Sie laufen geschwind mit dem
Schaf von ihrem Raum, geradeaus zum heiligen **Stall.**

Dritte
Die Englein knieten vor dem Kindlein nieder, und ver-
sprachen, daß sie kämen balde wieder. Und draußen, bei ihrem
Raum, dachten sie, was soll das werden, daß arme Kind halb
bekleidet in der ... liegt, von den ...

Das Christkindlein in der **Krippe** liegt,
von den **Engeln** sanft gewiegt, von **Maria** und **Josef**
treu bewacht, denn es war eben aus dem Himmel gebracht.

wage, has long been much appreciated. It is not just a Christmas present in the eyes of the law. It constitutes an additional element in wages paid by the employer at Christmas. Length of employment is important here, and Christmas money is only paid to people who have worked for a specific period for a firm.

Some branches of industry and trade are so caught up in the Christmas rush that you might think this single festivity determines weal and woe for the entire year. That is in fact the case for the book trade and for the producers of Christmas cookies. Anyone who has experienced how some people have to work right up to the last minute on Christmas Eve will know all about that. Postmen rush to complete their deliveries, sales staff hardly have a moment's peace, and public transport gets more and more crowded from year to year. The last Christmas trees, already somewhat dishevelled, are sold, and flower shops are virtually ransacked. The festival of Christmas, inclusive of associated days for giving presents and the weeks up to Twelfth Night, has become a highly important economic factor. This festival thus plays a crucial part in public life.

Recipients of Christmas wishes

To return to the list once again. When ready, it is put in an envelope, addressed to the Christ Child (or in Northern Germany to Father Christmas), and left, in accordance with custom, on the window-sill. You sprinkle a little sugar on the letter just to make sure the Christ Child does not miss it. This letter is left out one evening about four weeks before Christmas, and the following morning the children rush to see if it has been taken. It sometimes happens though that this list of wishes lies around for a day, which is a great disappointment. What has happened? Well, parents and teachers want to increase the excitement, and also to indicate that presents should not be taken for granted and have to be earned. It is not surprising that old people tell youngsters: "If you're not good, you'll get nothing from the Christ Child". Such warnings are taken seriously — but, all the same, children have only one thought in their heads: Christmas. They have long since stuck colourful silver stars to their windows to show the Christ Child the way. School holidays start a few days before Christmas too.

For years now, resourceful local authorities have accepted letters sent to the Christ Child by post in order to be able to surprise the little petitioner with a present or some mark of regard. "The Kevelaer tourist office accepts letters to the Christ Child" — ran

33

an announcement in a Lower Rhine newspaper. "That is good news for all children aged up to twelve. Send your wishes by letter (Don't forget the stamp!) to the Christ Child, Post Box 201, 4178 Kevelaer, or simply put your letter in the box at the Kevelaer council offices in the Market Place. Your letters will be collected until December the 15th. On Saturday the 17th of December, St. Nicholas will be at the Kevelaer Market Place to open and read out 50 of your letters. Perhaps you will be among the lucky ones".

Children established this custom after the Second World War. When postal codes were introduced, they discovered the existence of a number of places from where Christmas post would certainly be sent on to heaven. There is a place in Northern Germany called Himmelreich (Kingdom of Heaven), and the post office there is deluged with more and more children's letters from year to year. The same thing happens at Himmelstadt in Southern Germany and Himmelstür in the Harz mountains. What were post office staff to do when confronted with a veritable mountain of wishes sent off in child-like trust?

It is not just children who express wishes either. Adults also have wishes which they convey, whether asked or not, to their partner, grown-up children, or relatives. The custom of giving money — Here, buy yourself something! — has crept in here and there but is frowned upon. Tradition demands a present, and giving should entail a surprise even though the recipient may perhaps reckon with whatever is involved. A present on Christmas Eve should be a token of personal thought and consideration, a carefully chosen expression of commitment and affection.

That still involves traces of Julklapp as Christmas is called by many families in Northern Germany. This is a special kind of surprise rather than a heathen custom, despite its Ancient Nordic origins. On Christmas Eve, the door of the room in which the family is sitting mysteriously opens, just enough for nuts, parcels, and presents to be thrown through the chink as if by magic. When the parcels are opened, they are found to contain an indication that they are meant for someone else. This person may not be the final recipient either. The parcel gets smaller and smaller, passing from hand to hand until it finally does reach the right person. You are not meant to know from whom the gift comes. The present must remain a real surprise if it is to retain its value as bringer of good fortune.

"Julklapp"

The Christ Child Market in front of Nuremberg's Frauenkirche.

VI.

Cards, Presents, and Their Distribution

Until they are about ten, children are much preoccupied with the question of who brings the presents at Christmas. This is a serious business. To say "I hope you don't still believe in the Christ Child" is not a theological injunction. What is involved is an attitude to life. To say that someone still believes in the Christ Child and in Christmas is viewed as meaning he or she is still a child, ruled by wishful thinking. For our children, of course, such a judgement is not derogatory. Mysterious things are happening all around in the time from St. Nicholas' Day to New Year, and children devote much energy and effort to solving these mysteries. The adults whisper together, and in larger houses a room remains locked. The presents are kept in this room away from both the children and the adult members of the family. About ten days before Christmas the children go to the woods to look for moss, and then spread it out to dry in the cellar, on the balcony, or somewhere else warm. All of a sudden this moss has disappeared. There is only one explanation for that — the Christ Child needs it for a crib. Then suddenly on Christmas Eve there stands a beautiful, decorated Christmas tree in the living room, and the children did not notice how it got there. "The Christ Child must have brought it" or "Father Christmas left it there" are the usual explanations of these events.

Where do presents come from — a crucial question

Come Christmas, newspapers and magazines start discussing this situation once again. There have long been two opposing educational trends. One demands that young people should accustom themselves to the realities of life at a sufficiently early stage. In other words, none of this hide-and-seek with the children. They should instead be given insights into daily life, including the fact that the money for Christmas gifts must be earned by sweat of the brow before parents or anyone else can give presents. We also live today in an enlightened age, and miracles only exist in the Bible. It is argued that children should not be treated as if they were stupid. They know more than they admit. The other camp wants to preserve for young people a wonderful, creative, and elevating experience. Only someone who has experienced this in childhood is capable in later years of cultivating this, passing it on, and utilising it in human relations. Adherents of this view express their opposition to the spiritual impoverishment of children in a world that needs love and desire for peace. They say that only people who had an experience like Christmas in its broadest sense are capable of this. These youthful experiences are later a rich possession and a constant source of creative action. The proof for that is to be found in the festival at issue, in Christmas itself.

This dispute extends to the books used at school. Should there be special reading-matter for Christmas or not? Is it not all too sweet, too sugary, too sentimental? And every year a broad section of the public expresses its views on this topic, directly or indirectly. Most people in our country want to celebrate Christmas in the traditional way with surprising presents, with songs and lights, with cosiness and memories of youth when one still believed in the Christ Child.

St. Barbara's Day (December the 4th) The time of surprising presents begins in some parts of the country with St. Barbara's Day on December the 4th — for children at any rate. Cherry branches are put in water so that they blossom at Christmas. Children can also put out a shoe that evening. When the little ones go to bed, they leave a shoe by their bed or near the stove or central heating. Once they are fast asleep, a member of the family puts some chocolate, biscuits, an apple, or something or other to eat in these shoes. Such shoes are of course beautifully clean, and perhaps also lined with a piece of cloth or a paper serviette. In the morning there is a general rush to the shoes. Parents may put out shoes too, and these also contain something or other so as to keep up appearances. If children are asked where these presents come from, they either do not know or answer: St. Nicholas. As we have already seen though, he does not arrive on earth until the following evening, and his festival falls on December the 6th.

That custom originally took place in the name of St. Barbara, the patron saint of miners, but she has been largely forgotten except in association with the cherry branches named after her. Her name may have been preserved in real mining areas but among the population as a whole the custom only survives as described above.

St. Nicholas' Eve (December the 5th) Then comes the 5th of December. On the evening of the 5th, Nicholas comes down to earth. Much has already been said about Nicholas in a separate section — including the fact of a particularly close link with this evening.

Das Christkindlein. | Le présent de Noël

"The Christ Child" — coloured print, 1840.

Father Christmas

Advertising makes great use of the figure of Father Christmas, which is basically a lay form of St. Nicholas. We encounter him on posters, at the entrance to big department stores, and at Christmas markets in the form of the Anglo-American Santa Claus. He has a white, flowing beard, and a red, fur-trimmed cap. His capacious coat is also red with fur trimmings, and his pockets are filled with dolls, toys, and canes. The figure of Ruprecht has completely vanished in East Germany over the years, and Nicholas – or Father Christmas – now appears alone.

The Christ Child

South of the river Main, gifts are still brought by the Christ Child, who very, very seldom ever appears. He does not even make an appearance on Christmas Eve despite frequent mention of his name between St. Nicholas' Day and Christmas. According to mothers, the Christ Child is omnipresent but never to be seen. In just a few areas in the Hunsrück, along the Nahe, in the Palatinate, and in distant Lausitz, the Christ Child does, however, go through the village on Christmas Eve. He enters houses where people have previously requested this, and distributes presents in the same way as St. Nicholas.

A letter from Theodor Storm to Gottfried Keller

"Hademarschen-Hanerau, 22nd December 1882

Here I am, dear friend, to shake your hand — as far as that is possible across such a great distance — to mark what for me is an eternally young childhood festivity. Downstairs my youngest is playing all kinds of sweet melodies, and everything is very Christmasy throughout the house. Done nothing for two days except pack boxes and make parcels, and send letters to old and young all over the place. This time I only have my two youngest, Gertrud and Dodo, at home, and tomorrow my Musicus, my music teacher, is coming from Varel. The broad-branched, twelve foot fir is already standing in the big room, and we have been hard at work in recent evenings. The golden fairy-tale branch, the cluster of alderberries, big fir cones to which life-size papier-maché crossbills will be clinging this time whilst two robins sit alongside their nest and eggs in the fir sprigs, and delicate white nets whose contents are carefully wrapped in gold and other coloured paper — Everything is ready, and tomorrow I will help decorate the room.

When the lights burn on Christmas Eve though and the children start their carol, I am overcome. Where are they all who were once happy with me? Answer: where I will soon be too. And the fate of those dear to you? An eternal darkness for you . . .

May the fairy-tale-like tranquillity of this festival descend on you

The "Gift-Bringing Child" among the Sorbs in the Lausitz area is a particularly impressive Christ Child. Clad in national costume and with the face veiled, it goes around at Christmas distributing presents. (Wolf Lücking)

too, no matter whether from the child in the crib or from our ancient, beautiful Goddesses . . ."

Distribution of presents on Christmas Eve

The shops shut punctually at 1 p.m. on December the 24th. There are, of course, public services that still have to be manned. Trams and trains must run, doctors continue to care for the sick, and urgent automobile repairs have to be carried out, but in general work stops at midday on Christmas Eve. Everyone makes their way home as quickly as possible so as to change for the festivity. You put on your best clothes for Christmas Eve. That is important. The small children sit in a corner, trying to conceal their impatience.

As soon as evening has come and the first Church bells sound out for Christmas Vespers, the distribution of presents gets under way in the family. The father or mother will have crept unnoticed into the locked room. A little bell is used to indicate that the Christ Child or Father Christmas has called and left presents for everyone. In homes where a locked room is not available for a longer period, all the members of the family are kept out of one room for at least this afternoon so that last-minute preparations can be made in feverish haste. When the bell sounds, the youngest is charged with opening the door to see what the Christ Child has brought. The door is opened, and there is a hush as everyone stops to admire the radiant tree. Such an occasion provides a demonstration of what light can — and used to — signify for man. In most families, particularly where there are children and young people, it is then customary to sing a pious song. The order of events is similar wherever Christmas Eve is traditionally celebrated in Germany. Only when this song is over may presents be unpacked and looked at. That is the moment that the children, large and small, have eagerly awaited for so long. Older members of the family time and again enjoy the pleasure of their children and other recipients of presents.

As soon as the presents have been distributed, one of the children will be asked to say a poem. Someone from the family will sit down at the piano and play carols. Where that is not possible, the family will listen to Christmas records or a Christmas concert on the radio. Come what may, there must be music on Christmas Eve.

Families differ as to whether they have their Christmas meal before or after the distribution of presents. In many Catholic households it is still customary to eat little throughout the day. The 24th used in fact to be a day of fasting. In most regions there are very specific dishes for Christmas Eve. On Christmas Day most people have a goose, a dish originally associated with St. Martin's Day. In south-

Christmas in pietistic circles in the year 1834 — aquarelle by Ludwig Emil Grimm, whose brothers, Wilhelm and Jacob, collected the celebrated fairy tales.

erly parts of Germany, south of a line from Munich to Passau, the main meal on Christmas Eve follows the Midnight Mass. The main element here is a kind of consommé with dumplings.

The presents

A great diversity of presents are given in the Federal Republic but they can be divided up into categories. Items of clothing continue to occupy the first place, articles that one must have anyway and are necessary because of the cold at this time of year. Older people are more likely to give one another something practical. In poorer times people were happy if they got just a little something on Christmas Eve, and the war years taught people such modesty. Only in recent years when affluence spread did people start to adopt a different attitude to the giving of presents. They have increasingly resorted to presents that do not necessarily serve any practical function. Electrical goods are now much in favour: television sets, computers and CD players, even musical instruments, and cameras, projectors, and ever more elaborate accessories. All kinds of sports equipments have also become popular presents. The car makes it possible to get to winter sports areas relatively quickly, and a large number of skating rinks have been set up in densely populated areas, so skiing equipment, skates, and the necessary clothing are now favourite presents among the young and the middle-aged.

On the other hand, individually produced presents, which were much in evidence between the wars and even up to around 1955, are increasingly out of fashion. Knitted socks or gloves, a self-made lamp-shade, a photo album full of souvenir pictures, and enamel-work produced at evening courses expressed the donor's feelings. Such presents were often little things, a book-mark, a calender, or a ribbon, but they were treasured and preserved.

The significance of giving presents

People are now beginning to realise once again that a present bought in a matter of minutes does not do sufficient justice to Christmas. More and more people are pointing out the undesirable consequences of the way we regard the giving of presents. Children and young people get the idea that things will always continue like this. Increasing the value of presents is only possible to a limited extent though. What worries the critics even more, however, is that young people become accustomed to this idea of Christmas, viewing it as a festival of present-giving whose existence is more or less fortuitous. The heart of the Christmas message — "Peace on earth and goodwill to all men" — gets lost. So too do the feelings and the emotions involved in this festival.

That is why Churches of all denominations and the big welfare organisations are increasingly preoccupied by these disturbing

Der Struwwelpeter

oder

lustige Geschichten
und drollige Bilder

Wenn die Kinder artig sind
kommt zu ihnen das Christkind;
wenn sie ihre Suppe essen
und das Brot auch nicht vergessen,
wenn sie, ohne Lärm zu machen,
still sind bei den Siebensachen,
beim Spaziergehn auf den Gassen
von Mama sich führen lassen,
bringt es ihnen Guts genug
und ein schönes Bilderbuch.

The "Christ Child" from "Struwwelpeter".

developments. They call on the public to show concern for their neighbours, for anyone who needs help and suffers particularly much at Christmas from loneliness, poverty, and destitution. One such fund-raising activity is called "Adveniat" , thus making apparent the link with Christmas. These efforts should not be underestimated since readiness to give is never so great as at Christmas. The generositiy does not just apply to close relatives and personal friends. The German postal services have more to do at Christmas than at any other time of the year. There are quite a few people whose greatest pleasure at Christmas consists of giving to others. That is sufficient compensation for all the walking, waiting, and buying involved. From the start of Advent, all of human life is involved in activities devoted to love of neighbour and the giving of presents. Even organisations for the protection of animals are particularly concerned about wild creatures at Christmas, especially song-birds which have difficulties in finding food when snow falls early.

Religious services on Christmas Eve

Back to Christmas Eve though. When the distribution of presents is over, carols have been sung, and the dinner has taken place, peace returns to the family. People devote themselves to their presents, and pass the time sociably until midnight. Christmas services are held at midnight in both the Protestant and the Catholic Churches. Clergymen concede that these are the only services of the year when the Churches are overcrowded with people flocking to hear the gospel message of the birth of Christ. Churches in popular ski resorts are full too. Skiers may be mainly interested in enjoying Christmas in the snow but they do not want to miss the service in a village church. Until recently the Catholic mass was at 6 a.m. on Christmas morning.

If older people in Germany were asked about their most lasting impressions of Christmases long ago, over 90% would surely answer: "the Christmas Mass". All the church bells sound out to celebrate the start of the service. "Bells with holy sound through the world resound" — runs a Christmas carol. Hundreds of paintings and sketches by famous and lesser known artists depict people coming from all sides through the night to the Church with its illuminated windows. Churches serving scattered settlements particularly inspired such pictures with churchgoers, carrying lanterns to find their way through the dark, surrounded by snow. Our Christmas cards have seized on this motif all too eagerly.

Equally many poets and writers have recorded the way taken to Midnight Mass in their poems and stories. They may approach this subject from a diversity of religious or non-religious attitudes but their narratives have one thing in common. Strange occurrences,

Christmas Mass at Cologne Cathedral.

which cannot be rationally explained, take place during this night. This belief is shared with large sections of the population. The ideas that come to light here must date far back to a time when the winter solstice still struggled with the birth of Christ for predominance and the allegiance of believers.

The Churches are festively decorated. Everything is bathed in light, and the altars are flanked by fir trees — with and without decorations — whose fresh resin disseminates a spicy aroma. Graphic depictions of the birth of Christ are even to be found in many Protestant Churches, particularly in the Erzgebirge, the centre of this faith's adherence to Christmas customs. Light, song, and the words of the Gospel characterise the service. In many places, a custom has developed of ending the service with everyone singing "Silent Night, Holy Night". Another favourite song employed for this purpose starts: "O happy, o blessed Christmas".

Christmas in Thuringia by Johannes Keßler

"Christmas, O Christmas, Highest of Days,
Uncomprehending, its bliss we extoll.
In its holy veil enfolded,
Secure the most blessed secret stays".

Lenau gave those words to his Savonarola, and we also, time and again, experience Christmas as the highest of days, the festivity of the Highest and the Most Glorious, of Love, of Divine and Human Love. That is why for some people Christmas festivities constitute the highpoint of their lives coupled with unforgettable memories.

When I think back to what has remained the first clear-cut memory from my earliest childhood, it is a memory of Christmas. I still see before me the little Thuringian village of Bröckau, deep in snow. Mother wakes us three children. Even though it is still dark outside, sleep is quickly rubbed out of our eyes. It is Christmas morning! We are to go to the Christmas mass! My mind still sees the picture: father in his robe, mother taking my two sisters by the hand, our faithful Marie leading the way with the lantern. Thus we go to the little village church, greeted by old and young. The church is much too small at this moment. Anyone who is not ill in bed is on the move. The most important moment for us children came when we entered the little church. This simple, old House of God had no lighting system but every churchgoer had brought a candle, lit this, and fixed it in position with some drops of wax. This flickering sea of lights was an unforgettable picture. It was not the beauty of the scene that most pleased us scoundrels though. We were much more fascinated by whose light fell over and how the damage was made good. On the altar stood the mysterious Christmas picture. And then came the most exciting moments. While my father read the Christmas story, the sexton behind this

Christmas at the home of Annette von Droste-Hülshoff, the authoress of such novellas as "Die Judenbuche", known far beyond Germany (from "Jenny's Skizzenbuch").

transparent image lit one light after another, and at the moment of the Christmas message — 'For unto you is born this day a Saviour which is Christ the Lord' — the picture revealed the Holy Family, the shepherds, the ox, and the ass in full glory. Breathlessly, I followed these fairy-tale-like developments, and my mother had to hold me back from pushing forward to the altar. In these moments I was so proud of my father and his ability to give orders like God — 'Let there be light!' It was then that there arose, for the first time, the wish to become a clergyman too so that I could one day conduct the Christmas service. And when, decades later, I did conduct a Christmas service — on Christmas Eve rather than early on Christmas Day — in my Potsdam garrison church with the orphans' choir and the guardsmen's trombones, in St. Lukes at Dresden with a beautiful, big crib embellished with wood-carvings before me and a packed congregation of thousands, and in the field, whether in Lille cathedral or in sheds, barns, and dug-outs along the Dvina, I thought of how the wish of the small pastor's son in a little village church had been so richly fulfilled".

(Taken from: Thüringer Hefte 11—12/1960. Reprinted by kind permission of the publisher)

Christmas greetings Silence is largely maintained on the way to the church, but once the service is over acquaintances wish one another "Happy Christmas". Children are also encouraged to greet neighbours and friends in this fashion.

That provides an opportunity for mention of another sphere of human contact at Christmas. Christmas is the only time of year when you have to write to all your friends and relations. There are people who only go to church at Christmas, and there are equally many who only send written greetings to friends, relatives, colleagues at work, and superiors and subordinates on this occasion. Perhaps you see the person concerned every day or perhaps not at all — the Christmas card must be written and Christmas greetings despatched.

Many German writers, painters, and composers wrote Christmas letters which have since been included in Christmas books as providing a vivid picture of their age and selves.

The Christmas card has established itself in Germany as in many other countries. Such greetings as "Merry Christmas and a Happy New Year" save the writer work. Christmas card designs are well-known: a snow-covered mountain landscape, a lit candle on a Christmas tree, the birth of Christ, the adoration of the shepherds, and the Three Wise Men. Post-card size aquarelles and drawings,

Christmas during the "Wilhelminian era". This drawing from "Die Kleine Presse" (24. 12. 1894) shows the high spirits prevalent in middle class circles.

devoted to either secular or religious themes, are also very popular. Fir trees in the snow are just as indispensable as the bell in the church tower.

Do greetings bring good fortune?

The great care devoted to expressing Christmas greetings, usually coupled with best wishes for the New Year, indicates that such greetings are intended to bring good fortune to the recipient. It is not a matter of chance that this idea of bringing good fortune is set in the time between the old and the new years. This period between Christmas and Twelfth Night has long been viewed as particularly propitious and as a time for looking into the future. If a greeting is expressed and received during this time, the hope is that the recipient will get through the new year without illness or personal difficulties.

All the peoples of our earth know of these wishes for a healthy and happy new year. All these peoples have times of year when their wishes stand particularly good chance of fulfilment. Amid their wealth of fairy stories and other tales, there are always invocations of the times when wishes helped. All these tales stipulate particular times of day and year as the indispensable precondition for fulfilment of wishes — and for us that is the time between Christmas and Twelfth Night.

The following excerpt from Emil Barth's wartime diary provides an example of determination — despite the most adverse of circumstances — to celebrate Christmas and its significance. Christmas in Germany reaches down to the roots for everyone.

Emil Barth's Christmas 1944

"Christmas Eve yesterday. Not even a gesture of respect was thought necessary for the spirit of this festival. A long and oppressive stay in the cellar during extensive air attacks and the earth continuously shaken by massive bombing. What terrible lessons!

Despite all my grief, I must tell myself though that a year ago I scarcely dared hope I might still be able to spend this year's festival here in an undamaged home. We have decorated the room with branches — from the tree known as Arbor vitae which might be from the grave of our most recent loss, and from the thorny green of holly, the wild laurel, which we gathered in the wood, evoking so many dear and productive memories for me.

The family assembled later at the beautiful festive table upstairs in the old house. Substitutes, as it were, had also been invited in place of absent members of the family. At the last moment, a young wounded, homeless soldier had managed to get hold of a fir tree. The candles burnt there as if for departed souls. We followed the old custom and sang "Silent Night", so familiar from childhood. Some voices were almost overcome by tears at the thought of the fallen, the vanished, and those far away. Only now do I realise the significance of that flood which in my July 1938 dream swept over our continent, drifting along like an ice floe, and understand that it wanted to presage that generals and troops were still on the march with their tattered banners on this sinking ice floe, rammed by the bows of an advancing ship, shadowy and mighty!"

(Published by kind permission of Frau Erika Barth, Düsseldorf).

The Second Day of Christmas (St. Stephen's Day)

Boxing Day is very much a day for paying visits. Relatives go to one another's houses, or come together for an afternoon with the oldest member of the family. They tell one another about their presents and the experiences of Christmas Eve, and view their host's acquisitions and tree.

Here Karl Arnold, the celebrated caricaturist from "Simplizissimus",
the satirical magazine, shows great understanding of Joachim Ringel-
natz's "Seaman Kuttel Daddeldu's Christmas celebration", dating
from the mid-1920s.

The 26th is also a day when some families go with their children
to the church to look in peace at the crib there. The evening is
devoted to going to the theatre, and to the special Christmas
meetings of sports clubs.

52

On the second day of Christmas, the Catholic Church comme-
morates St. Stephen, the first martyr, which is why the 26th is
known as St. Stephen's Day. A parade takes place in areas where
horse breeding flourishes and riding clubs are popular. The riders
say that the horses need exercise and have to be taken out. That
is of course true, but behind that is an old custom. St. Stephen is
also viewed as a source of help against animal diseases. Horse
blessings still take place in Bavaria, Westphalia, and the Lower
Rhine area. The horse stands for all livestock here, and is blessed
in the hope that this will keep away diseases and epidemics.

VII.

Plants, Flowers, and Trees for Christmas

Advent starts on the first Sunday after November the 26th. This time is devoted to preparations for Christmas. After the four Advent Sundays are over, there follow Christmas Eve and Christmas Day. It can happen that the fourth Sunday in Advent and Christmas Eve fall on the same day.

The Advent calendar

Almost everything that happens during the Advent period is done with Christmas in mind. If a house-painter has a job, it is expected this will be completed before Christmas Eve, and other more extensive projects have to be completed by then too.

Advent calendars with their bright Christmasy pictures hang alongside children's beds. If you look more closely, you discover small numbers in this picture. One, two, three, and so on up to 24. Wherever the numbers are, there are small paper windows. When you open these windows you find a little picture on transparent paper: a candle, a ball, a snowman — whatever children like. They open a new window every morning, and then they know that there are still twenty three days to Christmas, twenty two, twenty one, and so on. Every day Christmas Eve, so much longed for and charged with wishes, comes a little closer. These Advent calendars can also be stood on the table in front of a lit candle so that the little windows are illuminated to children's great delight. A more recent variant of the Advent calendar consists of a chain of candles. Small balls of wax or stearin are numbered one to twenty four for the days till Christmas, and one of these is lit and burns down every evening. Care must be taken of course to ensure that this candle-chain not cause any risk of fire.

The Advent star is a special form of Advent calendar. Twenty four little stars are attached to a big six-pointed star. A little star is removed every day until on Christmas Eve the unadorned large

Advent stars

star hangs on the wall as a symbol of the light associated with the days to come.

Advent stars based on the model established by the Bohemian Brethren have also become popular. This is a free-standing star that can have 20, 26, 30, 50, or even 110 points. It disseminates an auspicious light — maybe red, or some other colour — through-out the whole of Advent. The Brothers at Bad Boll sell such stars so as to perform charitable works with the proceeds.

Advent wreath   Apart from the Advent calendar, families also have an Advent wreath. This is a wreath made out of bound fir twigs to which four candles are attached. One more candle is lit for each of the Advent Sundays. In large houses, shops, and in Churches, these Advent wreaths hang from the ceiling, adorned with four fat red or yellow candles. This looks particularly splendid when the wreath is also decorated with red or violet ribbons dangling pic-turesquely. The time of contemplation, of family togetherness, has started. In many places, church and secular groups hold a splendid celebration around the first Sunday in Advent. Choirs perform Advent songs, and music is played in the family circle. The Advent wreath is on the table in most homes. As it gets dark on the Sunday afternoon, the father, mother, or one of the older children takes a book and reads some poems or a story. The small ones listen in complete silence, heads on their arms and eyes fixed on the candles. Perhaps a boy or girl has learnt this poem by heart:

> Good tidings we bring of Advent's return.
> Look, the first candles already burn!
> Christians rejoice!
> Be of good cheer
> for the Lord is near!

As the wax drips onto the green twigs, the words or song fade away, and the season of Christmas really starts.

No-one knows when the Advent wreath came to Germany and where it originated. It does not date back very far as a Christmas custom but has already firmly established itself. If you happen to pass by flower shops or nurseries during the week before the first Sunday in Advent, you will see many, many Advent wreaths, and eager hands binding and decorating more wreaths. Pine and fir cones, little red mushrooms, or red and yellow ribbons are also attached to the green of the wreath. Here and there artificial snow is strewn on the twigs since winter is already under way.

Perhaps the Advent wreath came to Germany from Sweden in emulation of the nordic 'Crown of Lights'. It was originally more

"Föhr Arch" – a "frame-tree" with biscuit shapes: Adam and Eve, fish, cock, pig, cow, ship, and mill from the North Sea island of Föhr. (Collection Maud Pohlmeyer)

common in North German towns than elsewhere in the country. From around 1930 it suddenly spread to all levels of the population. You can easily make such a wreath for yourself, and anyone who cannot do that or does not find any fir twigs can be satisfied with a decorated candle whose pre-Christmas glow is almost equally good.

New Advent customs

There is a more recent custom linked with the Advent wreath. This was introduced within a very short time by long-distance lorry drivers, and has already spread throughout the Federal Republic and to neighbouring countries. At the start of Advent, these drivers put a small plastic Christmas tree in their cabins. The coloured bulbs on the tree are connected to the lorry's battery and lit up after dark.

Cherry branches for St. Barbara

An older-established group of workers, the mining community, cultivated and brought about the rapid spread of another custom. The 4th of December was and still is a special day for miners. As has already been mentioned, this is St. Barbara's Day. She became the patron saint of miners in commemoration of her painful martyrdom. Legend reports that her father, a heathen, did not want her to become a Christian. When he discovered that she had nevertheless gone ahead and acted against his will, he dragged her before the Roman tribunal which condemned Barbara to death. No-one was ready though to execute this delicate girl. Her enraged father then cut off Barbara's head himself. No sooner had he done this terrible deed than there was a mighty clap of thunder, and a flash of lightning out of a clear sky struck down this man who had murdered his own child. For that reason Barbara became patron saint of all vocations concerned with fire and explosions — the fire brigade, the artillery, and miners.

On the 4th of December, miners honour Barbara by putting freshly cut cherry, elder, or pear branches into a jug filled with water and keep this in a warm place. The branches must have vigorous buds so that they will blossom and turn green on Christmas Eve to the day. People say that when these branches do blossom for Christmas, misfortune will stay away from the house in the coming year.

Other Christmas greenery

The wish to have blossoms and fresh greenery in the house during the darkest days of winter signifies even more though. They act as a sign and a guarantee that autumn and winter will once again be succeeded by spring and summer. That is one reason why these branches for St. Barbara are to be found all over the Federal Republic. Holly *(Ilex aquifolium)* is a favourite means of decoration for Advent and Christmas in the west of Germany. Its dark-green,

Advent wreath with Advent calendar — as you can make for yourself.
In each of the little packets bearing a date there is a match-box, filled
with a little present for children or friends.

spiky leaves do not dry out so quickly, and the contrast with the
bright red berries is highly attractive.

The poinsettia *(Euphorbia pulcherrima)* is not native to Germany,
and is therefore a relative newcomer among Christmas plants.
It originally came from overseas but is now established in flower

shops and nurseries in Europe. The topmost young leaves on the plant take on a red or yellow hue around Christmas. These leaves are attached to the end of the stem like horizontal windmill sails, bringing colour and life into homes.

The Christmas Rose   There is no doubt though that the queen of all the flowers and plants that blossom for Christmas in northern parts of Central Europe is the Christmas Rose *(Helleborus niger)*. Its pinkish blossoms are even to be found amid snow and ice, and have been extolled by such writers as Eduard Mörike in many poems and stories. Tradition has it that this inconspicuous plant blossoms during Christmas Night when all other plants are covered by snow and awaiting spring. The Christmas Rose is also known as the Snow Rose or the Winter Rose. In earlier times, it was to be found in all farmers' gardens because its black roots provided an important cure for certain animal diseases. The fact that this is otherwise a poisonous plant increased the fascination of its blossoms. The Christmas Rose also played a part in the Germanic celebrations marking Midwinter Night.

Moss   Mention must also be made of moss, which serves an important function at Christmas, particularly in Catholic areas. Even though its use may have declined in large towns and settlements far away from woods, moss is still needed wherever there is a Christmas crib or a Christmas mount (as in Saxony). Boys still wander through the woods before Christmas gathering moss, which is then dried at home without losing its fresh green colour. This moss is used to represent woods, heathland, and, above all, the fields where the shepherds learnt of the miracle at Bethlehem.

Mistletoe   Germans have taken over the English custom of making mistletoe *(Viscum album)* a part of Christmas. Educated Germans know all about the significance of kissing under the mistletoe, and there is often a sprig hanging from the ceiling or door-frame. This plant was not unknown in Germany — as is shown by the names of witch or thunder broom given to it. It was not a part of Christmas though. Mistletoe was usually hung in the cow-stall to drive away evil spirits, and people in the lowlands of Northern Germany, along the Ems, in Hamburg, and in Pomerania were well aware of such powers. Nowadays though mistletoe is sometimes included in Advent wreaths, sprayed with gold or silver to glitter in the candle-light.

The Christmas tree   The undisputed focal-point of the entire Christmas period, in the community and in the family, is the Christmas tree. A German

Helleborus niger
flore viride.

The Christmas Rose from the "Hortus Eystettensis" of 1713.

Christmas without the green fir tree is simply inconceivable. The tranquil splendour of Christmas tree lights is an essential aspect of the festival for both the individual and the population as a whole. This green tree is above denominations and political parties, philosophies and ideologies. It is the symbol of Christmas for all Germans, who have to have their Christmas tree on December the 24th even if they live in South America or Africa, in the Middle or the Far East. Trees are also to be found in churches and public squares. They are used in shops as decoration, and in offices to please staff and visitors. There is a Christmas tree at airports, at railway stations, and in schools. No firm that thinks anything of itself would dare deprive its employees of their Christmas tree. Prisoners doing their daily round of exercise in gaol courtyards are greeted by a tree high up on the roof. Even during the war, soldiers in Africa and sailors on the high seas were not ready to be without a Christmas tree. Christmas and the Christmas tree are almost synonymous. The one would be deprived of content without the other.

Varieties of tree It should not be so but it is: the Christmas period gets under way with the tree's appearance, and is all of a sudden over when the tree is removed from the house again. Children want to keep the tree for as long as possible so as to stop this marvellous time coming to an end. It is hardly surprising that they view it as *the* tree rather than as a mere fir, pine, or whatever, decorated for Christmas. The more you direct attention towards these trees, the more individual they appear. There are slender trees with thin branches, and there are stocky trees with strong branches capable of supporting candles and decorations. If the tree is not strong enough, the candles quickly tip over and have to be put to rights time and again. Some families have a preference for silver firs, which are specially cultivated in nurseries. Others like blue spruce, which are very strong, grow absolutely straight, and bring variety and colour into the home with their distinctive appearance. There are a considerable number of forest owners who cultivate Christmas trees year in, year out. In October and early November, the foresters start to select the trees to be felled and transported in great loads to the towns.

The giant fir trees that stand in public places are specially grown for this purpose and carefully looked after in municipal woods. They are often up to 25 metres high. Large lorries and cranes are needed to get the tree set up on its Christmas site. Workmen are kept busy for a day securing the tree, and making use of fire brigade ladders to decorate it and fix the coloured lights. There are public places that have been virtually ennobled by the fact that the great town Christmas tree stands there year after year. These include the market place in Munich and the space in front

Christmas tree decoration from around the turn of the century.
Coloured lithograph from 1890.

of the Old Town Hall in Bonn. The same tree, a mighty fir growing in front of the former town hall, is used every year at Wermels-kirchen east of Cologne, and is ideal for this purpose. A slender fir has flourished for decades on the castle ruins above the town of Virneburg near the Nürburgring racing circuit in the Eifel, and the local people are particularly proud of their living Christmas tree. And those are only just a few examples of how important the Christmas tree has become for us.

Origin of the festive tree

Scholars have long been concerned with the origins of the Christ-mas tree. How long has the custom of having a tree at Christmas been established? Well, Otto Lauffer, author of the most reliable book on the Christmas tree to date, writes: "At no time during early Germany history (inclusive of Scandinavia and England) or during the centuries of the Christian Middle Ages was there a festive tree to mark Mid-Winter or the Christian Christmas Festival. There is no written or visual record of such a tree before the 16th century". Pictures showing Martin Luther together with his family in front of a candle-lit tree were, unfortunately, produced centuries later.

The Evergreen

The 'evergreen' existed at a very early date in the west of Ger-many including Alsace and parts in Switzerland. Lights (again in general terms) were to be found to the east of line drawn from Bremen to Nuremberg. Only when these two customs merged — as was the case everywhere in Protestant areas — was the Christmas tree, complete with candles, established. That was not so long ago either. In 1708 Duchess Elisabeth Charlotte of Orléans, writing to her daughter, the Duchess of Lorraine, described a game called "Christi Child". "Tables are set up like altars with all kinds of things for every child: new clothes, silver trinkets, dolls, sweetmeats, and anything you can imagine. Box bushes are put out on these tables with a candle fixed to every branch. This looks absolutely charming . . ." We do not know whether this took place in the Palatinate court at Heidelberg or at Hanover — both Protestant courts.

Almost all early testimony to the festive fir points to the south-west, to Alsace, and, above all, to Strasbourg. A manuscript dating from 1605 says: "At Christmas, people in Strasbourg set up fir trees in their rooms with roses cut from multi-coloured paper, apples, cakes, tinsel, and sugar hanging from the branches . . ." Some-what later a preacher in the same town, Johann Conrad Dann-hauer by name, complained: "Among the trifles to which people often devote more attention than to the Word of God in celebrat-ing the old Christmas is the Christmas or fir tree, which is set up at home, hung with dolls and sweets, and finally ransacked".

These "Hanging Lights" (from Wunsiedel) for long took the place of a "fir tree" in the Fichtelgebirge area. It was only this century that this variety of Christmas Pyramid became a museum-piece.

If you study old books and observations in greater detail, you come to the conclusion that what mattered was to have greenery in the house over Christmas. That might be box, yew, or holly. The intention — to simplify somewhat — was to counter deadly winter, seen as starting on December the 21st, with fresh life. People wanted to conjure up and to invoke life, fertility, and the wonder of the annual rebirth of nature. The same attitude is often expressed today in houses adorned everywhere with twigs and little trees for Christmas. That is a beautiful and probably very old custom, going back a long way in Swabia and the Palatinate. An old gentleman from Westphalia also records that "Here there are still a number of families that mark Christmas by bringing box bushes in pots into the house. Hazel nuts are fixed to branches, pointing upwards like little candles".

There is no longer any difference between religious denominations. The Palatinate and Swabia are Protestant, and the area of Westphalia around Cologne is Catholic. That means that the tradition of evergreens at Christmas touches on a very deep level of man's soul. Whether in England, North America, France, or Russia, people share this feeling with Germans. The symbols of life predominate during the days of Christmas, beyond denomination and ideology.

There are a number of regional variants. The preference in Thuringia and the Lower Elbe is for fir, around Oldenburg and in Switzerland for holly, and in Berlin and around Lippe for ivy. The tenacity of this tradition with its revelation of fundamental aspects of human existence becomes apparent in the account of a Bishop who died in Spain in 580 A.D. He felt it necessary to ban the adornment of houses with laurel and evergreens as a heathen practice. Around the year 1000 Bishop Burchard of Worms decreed the same ban for similar reasons, and a hundred years later Ivo of Chartres did the same in his diocese. Such bans had little effect or else Hans Jacob Christoph von Grimmelshausen would not have been able to tell in his novel "Simplizissimus" (around 1669) of little box bushes being given as New Year's presents.

The extent to which this old custom was permeated by ancient mythical ideas is demonstrated by the fact that in Baden (as reported by Johann Peter Hebel), the Palatinate, Swabia, and Switzerland this greenery is not put on the table or fixed on the wall. It is hung from the ceiling, particularly where beams cross — a place of great importance for the solidity of the house. The secret magical powers attributed to this greenery were meant to stop harm coming to the house. Even up to our time in rural areas of Thuringia where tradition was strong among some families, the Christmas tree still hung from the ceiling.

A "Barbara branch" as delighted young ladies in Berlin society around 1880.

The significance of light

And now light. The custom of setting out lights in Christmas night is even older than the tradition of greenery, and certainly more widespread throughout Central Europe. Lights were even put out with the cattle in their stalls despite the danger of fire. Light dispels blackness, night, and darkness. When light is absent during the dark nights of winter, man attempts to create it in his own way. If you study the old festivities in the pre-Christmas period, there are always references to light and fire. On St. Martin's Day big fires are lit, and processions of lights wend their way through villages and towns. The Crown of Lights consists of a crown of burning candles worn by the day's bride. The Advent calendar marks the transition of this tradition from the individual to the family. The increase in the number of candles lit as Christmas approaches testifies to the importance of light in this period.

This celebration of light was considerably furthered by the fact that the Church gave its support to this custom from an early date. The Church also marks the end of the Christmas period with a special festival, Candlemas on February the 2nd, when the emphasis is once again on light's power as a symbol of God's works.

Light and fire in every form are part of Christmas traditions. To-day's reader should be reminded though of the difficulties in-volved in having light in the home a hundred years ago. Sources of light were provided by wax which was very expensive, bad oil which only lit dimly, and pitch or resin which produced sparks and smoke. Most people could hardly ever afford real wax candles except at Christmas — and even then they had to scrape and save throughout the year in order to celebrate Christmas with a candle-lit tree. In such circumstances, people's pleasure in this celebration was doubled, and it meant much more to them. Cand-les were especially important for miners and they carved the most beautiful candlesticks for Christmas.

Christmas pyramids

In many parts of Germany where the green of spruce and fir was too expensive, people were satisfied with lights. The whole of the Erz Mountains area and extensive parts of Saxony became famous for their pyramids of lights. Rods of the same length are attached to each corner of a square piece of wood, and the other ends are tied together. That produces a pyramid. This has to be firmly based so three rows of transverse rods are used to strengthen the structure. The lights are attached to the protruding ends of these transverse rods.

That is the basically simple principle employed in construction of light pyramids. What is important though is that all the hopes and expectations invested in the approaching festival of Christmas

Christmas Candlebras from the Erzgebirge.

were expressed in the decoration of these pyramids. They were carved from good wood, painted, and embellished. The ends of the rods, serving as candle-holders, were carved as angels or as miners in their old costumes. A great variety of artistic combinations were devised to make these pyramids even more attractive, and some of them were made to be hung from the ceiling.

In Thuringia there was the hoop-tree. Three hoops were attached at regular intervals to a rod hanging vertically. The bottom-most hoop was the largest and the other two decreased in size so that their candles did not set fire to what was above. This form of decoration has almost died out today.

Pyramids, on the other hand, flourished remarkably in other parts of the country. In the Erz Mountains they were mainly made of wood, which could then be painted and carved. In other areas they were adorned with greenery. Box, ivy, fir, and holly were twisted around the supporting rods in Breslau and Pomerania, in Hamburg and Berlin. In the former capital these rods were also decorated with coloured paper instead of twigs, and Wilhelm Raabe described such a simple pyramid in his celebrated Berlin novel "Die Chronik der Sperlingsgasse" (1857). He saw these pyramids as the little man's Christmas tree, which is what they were. These simple wooden constructions were not thrown away either. After Christmas was over they were stored until the following year.

Such pyramids are also to be found today in Bavaria and the Rhineland. They are now often hung with bells which ring out when rising heat from the candles makes the pyramid start to revolve.

In the words of a German scholar: "The tree ultimately triumphed over the pyramid in a struggle involving history and customs". "The links between the tree's winter greenery and lights" remained — and still are — important. With this development, extending over almost two hundred years, scholars can be sure that nothing remains today of the original ideas about driving out spirits and invocation of a fruitful time of year.

Decorating the tree The tree must still be decorated though — as described in the letter by the Duchess of Orléans. In earlier times, candles were perhaps enough in the eyes ot children and adults. Today though everyone wants a well-decorated tree in their home. You can even say that there have been areas — such as Rhenish Hesse and the Spessart — where the sweets on the tree have been more important than the lights. People there spoke of a Sugar Tree rather than a Christmas tree, and this was hung with edibles and decorations. Families with children maintain this custom up to the present day.

The tradition of hanging apples and nuts in the tree is very much older, and also a lot cheaper. These nuts are painted silver and gold, or dipped in sugar, to make them more attractive. They are a part of Christmas in Scandinavia and in Northern Germany. St. Nicholas, Father Christmas, and the Christ Child all bring nuts. Roses cut out of coloured paper, tinsel, and biscuits or home-made animal figures also have a long history as Christmas tree decorations.

North German rope-tree from the age of sailing ships, serving sailors at sea as a Christmas tree.

The "Christ Child's Tree" as depicted in a "1795 Calendar of Miraculous Stories".

The Christmas tree underwent a fundamental change around 1880. Glass-makers in Thuringia discovered a new way of blowing glass balls, bells, and animals, and of silver-coating the inside surface. Silver tinsel was produced from tin-foil to hang over branches of the tree, and angels' hair, spangles, and silver stars were manufactured from glass-fibre.

Links between the tree and the Christian festival were established in the second half of the 18th century, particularly in Hamburg and Berlin. Here and there people started to hang a wax angel in the tree, and to decorate the topmost branch with a big golden star. Larger angels bore the inscription "Glory to God in the highest" in their hands.

The Christmas tree in the 1970s: "Old German".

Today every family has its own way of decorating the tree. Some families stick to nothing but candles, glass-balls, and tinsel. Others only employ straw stars and lights to beautify their trees. Innovations such as stars made from straw or wood shavings have also considerably helped producers of arts and crafts. There are familes which embellish their tree with red balls, red tinsel, and red candles. Others limit themselves to silver decorations with white candles. Families with children used to resort to electric candles so as to avoid fires but that almost belongs to the past again. Anyone who can afford it employs candles made from real bee's wax, which disseminate a marvellous aroma even though they may burn more quickly. Wherever there are children, sweets are once again hung in the tree. Lots are then drawn for these, or, not infrequently, they mysteriously vanish from the tree. Chocolate and marzipan rings are great favourites along with filled chocolates in the shape of nuts, bells, stars, or money.

Trees in the Church

The Catholic Church has played a special part with regard to Christmas greenery. It used of old to be completely opposed to this, presuming, not unjustly, that a great regard for greenery was a facade for heathendom and a relapse into pre-Christian customs.

Very much time passed before the Church allowed "Christ trees" (the only permissable name!) to be set up in churches. From the 13th and 14th centuries onwards, Catholics had taken over cribs from the Franciscan tradition as a substitute for greenery. When children in Protestant districts go and visit their playmates around Christmas, they say "We want to see your tree" whilst in Catholic areas they would still talk of wanting to see the crib. These differences are, of course, on the decline now, particularly in the big towns — and yet there are still many fathers who take their youngest to see cribs in local churches between Christmas and the New Year.

It was only recently therefore that the Christ or the Christmas tree was accepted in Catholic areas. This happened around 1900 in towns but took considerably longer in country districts. The tree only made its way in the hills on both sides of the Rhine after the First World War. Older village people report that they first experienced a Christmas tree in the home around 1930. It was even longer before the tree reached the last village church.

The Christmas tree around the world

The German Christmas tree made its way abroad at a much earlier date. The tradition of a decorated tree was taken to America by the many German immigrants. The tree was late in reaching France but established itself quickly. A German in Paris, Friedrich Hermann, reported in 1890 on how that came about. "A distribution of presents to poor children at the German St. Joseph's schools in Villette took place for the first time thirty years ago (1860). Two of the organisers had to go from domestic market to domestic market, hunted through the great market halls where the rarest products and most unusual goods are to be found, and went to the leading flower shops in order to get hold of a little fir tree that was scarcely three foot high. The seller said he had just taken the tree to market on the off-chance since he had to root it up anyway. He said he had once heard a vague story about the Germans' Christ tree at Christmas. In 1869 there were fir trees at most markets and even some at the chief flower shops. In 1890,

Christmas tree decorations popular for over 100 years.

several hundred and then thousands of trees were brought to the central market halls between the 10th and 15th of December, and some went to other markets and dealers too. Apart from the markets, some 300 dealers and shops in all parts of the city offered Christmas trees. Careful estimates indicate that between 30,000 and 35,000 were sold".

In England, the Christmas tree is said to have been taken up by the royal court around 1840. It arrived in Schleswig-Holstein, the most northerly part of Germany, as late as in Paris. It is quite clear that the larger towns were quicker to take up the Christmas tree. It was to be found in Berlin from 1780 onwards but it was over a hundred years before the tree penetrated as far as frontier areas.

The tree on Christmas Eve

Even today, parents arrange matters so that their three- to six-year-olds do not notice when the tree comes into the house. It often stands for a time in a little-used corner. The father and mother usually only put the tree in its proper place on the 23rd of December. Even then it is supposed to remain a secret from the children until Christmas Eve. The room is usually locked, and even when space is very limited in the home parents do all they can to keep the tree as a surprise for their children. This moment of surprise is extremely important for the Christmas festivity as a whole. Even though the children will have seen trees ablaze with light in towns, department stores, or in the neighbour's garden long before Christmas, the most beautiful and overwhelming impression is still provided by the moment when the lights are put out in the house and the door of the hitherto locked room is opened to reveal the family tree in all its radiance. Thousands of people travel long distances right up to Christmas in order to be present for this experience. It is certainly not easy for a non-German to comprehend this fundamental characteristic, uniting a degree of child-like naivety and sentimentality. Anyone who has really experienced it though will surely be able to understand why a Christmas song starts with the words:

"No finer tree in all the world
than Christ's tree of old".

VIII.

Songs and Music for Christmas

Christmas is not just talked and written about in Germany. Christmas is, above all, a time for singing and music-making. The festival is inconceivable without Christmas songs or Christmas music. There is constant mention at Christmas of the mysterious sounds of bells and other musical instruments, present in even the most modest of households.

A time for singing

This starts with the first Sunday in Advent and reaches an initial climax on Christmas Eve, the Holy Evening, when the silent night should be filled with sounds that seem to come from celestial spheres. A scholar has written of the season's religious songs that "The Christmas song is older than the festival of Christmas, and its oldest elements pre-date the birth of Christ". He bases his thesis on passages from the Bible, starting with Mary's song of praise after the Annunication — "My soul doth magnify the Lord, and my spirit hath rejoiced in God my Saviour". According to St. Luke, Zacharias, the father of John the Baptist, was the next to praise the Lord when his speechlessness vanished at his son's circumcision. We must imagine the Gospel sung as is the custom among pious Jews. "Blessed be the Lord God of Israel; for he hath visited and redeemed his people" — starts the old priest's song of praise. Next in St. Luke's Gospel follows the Angel's exultations in the fields of Bethlehem: "Glory to God in the highest, and on earth peace, good will towards men". During Christ's presentation at the temple, it is the old Simeon who starts to sing: "Lord, now lettest thou thy servant depart in peace, according to thy word. For mine eyes have seen thy salvation, which thou hast prepared before the face of all people".

Scholarship thus demonstrates that Christ's birth and childhood were accompanied by songs. Such spontaneous utterance is also a very important element in German songs for Christmas. On Christmas Eve, songs are sung when the door is opened, revealing the candle-lit tree. The excitement of young people, who have so

Songs for Christmas Eve

much looked forward to this day, finds release in the family singing Christmas songs together. These songs are of great importance — as is not the case at any other festivity, occasion, or time of year. There are, of course, differences from family to family, and in some places people are more musical than in others. These songs do not always have religious themes but they are all much concerned with Christmas. It is impossible to provide a survey of all the Christmas songs sung in Germany. That would demand a book of considerably over a hundred pages — and even that would not include all the songs that are still sung.

The oldest song

The Christmas song is, however, a very late arrival in homes and families. The oldest Christmas songs with a sustained melody are church music. The oldest carol that is still sung dates back to the 11th century, and has thus been sung in churches for 900 years. This starts with the words "Welcome Lord Christ, Lord of us all", and ends "Kyrie eleison — Lord have mercy on us". It was written down somewhere in the area between Aachen and Maastricht. The best-known, and one of the most recent, Christmas songs starts: "Silent Night, Holy Night". There we know the author of the text, the composer, the circumstances of composition, and where it was first performed.

Groups of songs

A degree of classification of German Christmas songs is perhaps important so as to bring out the nuances and differences. Advent songs are, of course, mainly sung at church services but they also play a part in other celebrations. They all serve the purpose of preparation for Christmas, and draw very much on the psalms. Even the most recent songs have preserved the basic religious character because they arose out of, and can only be comprehended in terms of, expectation of the Lord. "Rain down, o Heaven, the righteous man. Rain down, o clouds, the Redeemer". That is a fundamental theme during Advent, emphasised time and again during and after hard times. Advent was thus taken very seriously during the Second World War and the years immediately following. This celebration was a serious, contemplative occasion, very often linked with the sale of Christmas articles for charitable purposes, rather than a loud and cheerful festivity.

When people lack any sense of immediate urgency though, Advent songs take on an extremely worldly character.

"Tomorrow, children, is the day.
Tomorrow's the time for play".

Kirchenlied

auf die

heilige Christnacht.

für

Sopran und Alt

und

stiller Orgelbegleitung.

Text von Herrn Jos. Mohr Coadjutor.

comp. von Franz Gruber Schullehrer

in Arnsdorf und Organist in St. Nicola

oesterr. Laufen.

1818.

Facsimile of "Silent Night", the most celebrated Christmas song —
composer Franz Gruber's manuscript VII (around 1855).

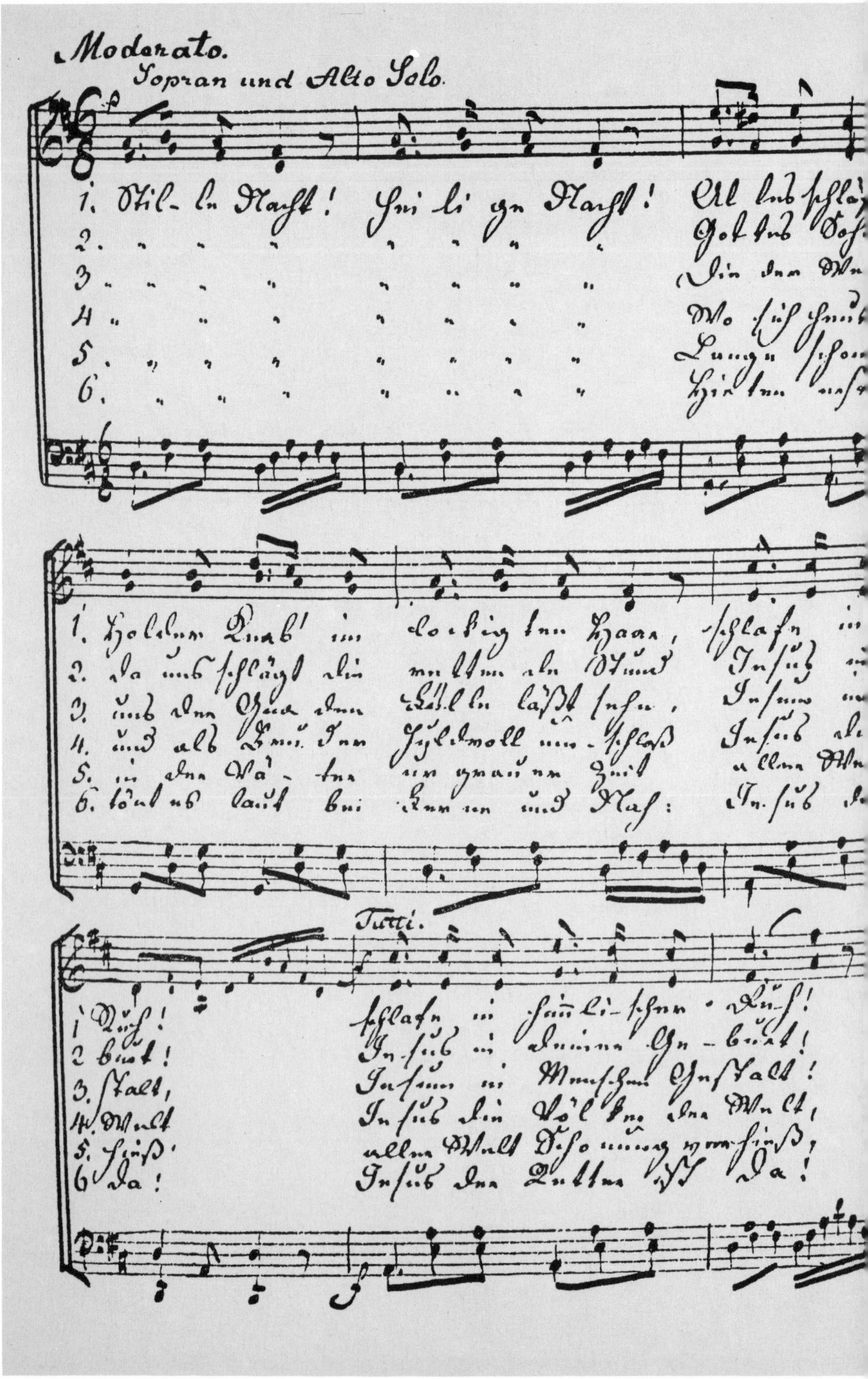
Moderato.
Sopran und Alto Solo
Tutti.

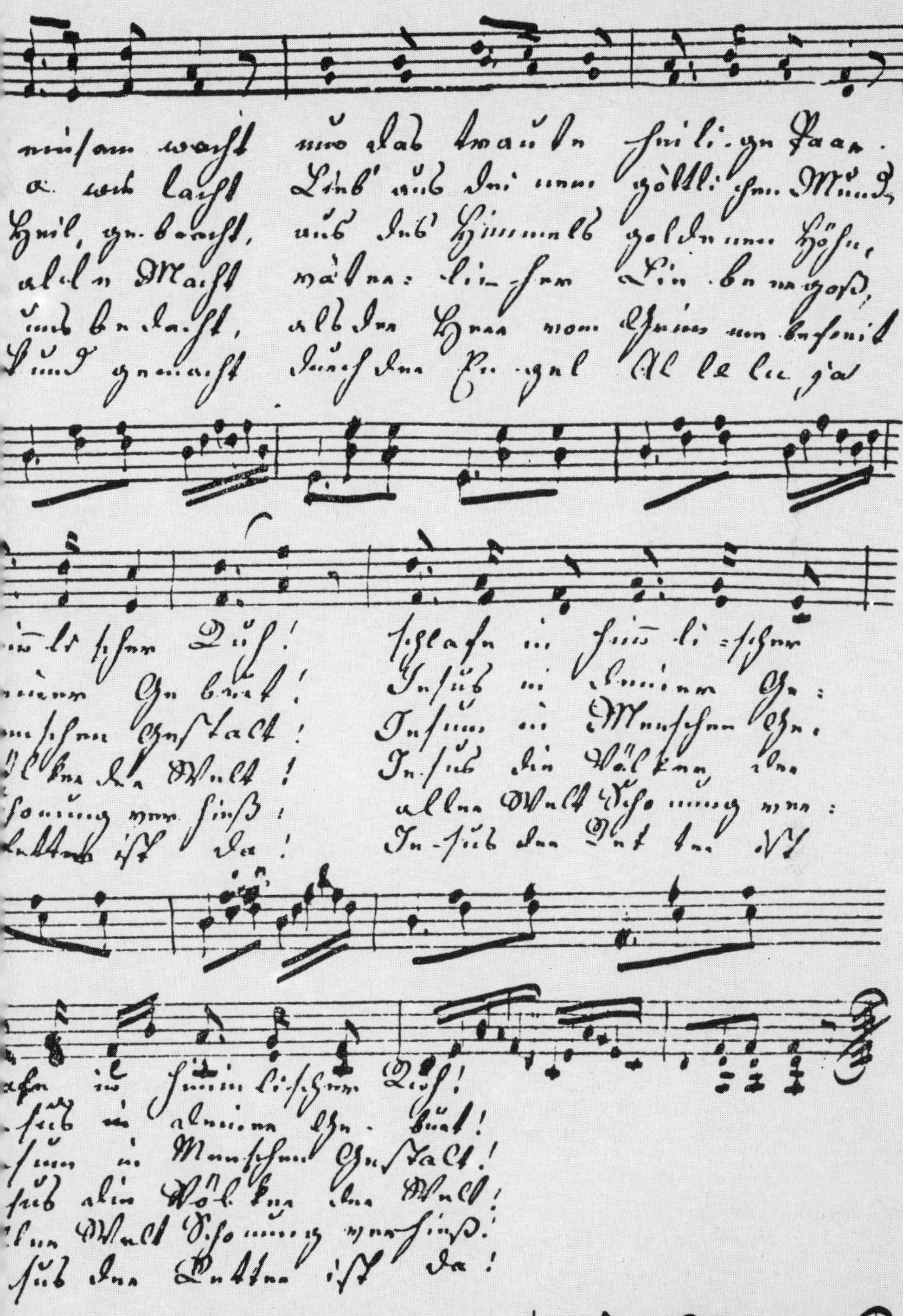

Advent songs are followed by Christmas songs, which can also be categorised in several groups. Firstly, there are the songs bringing tidings of great joy, headed by Martin Luther's celebrated "Vom Himmel hoch, da komm ich her" — words that Luther gives to the Angel that appeared to the shepherds.

Songs devoted to Mary and baby Jesus form a very large group. One of the oldest, dating from the 14th century, starts: "There is a flower springing, from tender roots it grows" (Es ist ein Ros' entsprungen) Mary is the rose referred to in the carol. Another favourite of choirs that sing folk-music begins:

"On the mountains blows the wind wild
and there cradles Mary her child".

These songs were originally sung without instrumental accompaniment.

Then there are the shepherds' songs, which are full of movement since these herdsmen were impelled to the crib by curiosity. These songs are happy and invigorating, encouraging people to follow the shepherds' example and rush to the crib:

"Come, all Christians, come apace,
Regard how the shepherds do race".

Such songs undoubtedly found a response among a population that until the 19th century lived from land and cattle. The herdsman was an important and respected man, particularly where animals were put out to pasture in the spring and stayed out until the start of winter enforced a return to the stall.

There are comparatively fewer songs concerned with the christening of Christ, the circumcision, and the Three Holy Kings from the East. The bones of the Three Kings have rested at Cologne since 1164 but the city has produced very few songs in their honour, and these have not established themselves either. Significantly, the songs devoted to the Three Kings in today's hymn books are of modern origin, the outcome of the revival of Epiphany carol singing after the Second World War.

Children's songs Children's songs for Christmas are also of recent origin, dating from around 1800. The best-known and most popular of them all starts:

"Come little children,
come all of you".

The last group is relatively recent too. This includes songs where the religious content has increasingly vanished. Such songs tell of bells that sound out more sweetly on Christmas Night than at any other time of year — or another starts:

"Little snow flake, clad in white,
where did you come from this snowy night . . ."

Others are concerned with fine presents or extol the Christmas tree: "O Tannenbaum, o Tannenbaum . . ."

Such songs can perhaps be called "Secular songs for Christmas". That sounds paradoxical since Christmas is, after all, hardly imaginable without its Christian elements. Nevertheless there are many people in our society who view Christmas as a secular celebration devoted to peace and joy, as a day which should be primarily devoted to the less fortunate. It is not easy to describe this "liberal" attitude that makes possible a "secular" Christmas. It is widespread though. Perhaps songs and music are so popular at Christmas because they can bridge opposites, and are understandable even without knowledge of the words.

When the festival of Christmas established itself in the Church centuries ago, there was not a great deal of singing. This was mainly left to the priests at the altar or the monks in large monastery churches. We know, for instance, that during the investiture of a Bishop in Prague the clergy sang "We praise thee O God", the nobility "Grant us mercy, o Christ, Kyrie eleison — and may all the Saints help us, Kyrie eleison". And the populace added their Kyrie eleison (Lord have mercy on us!). This same appeal is to be found in the oldest surviving Christmas song, which the judges of Aachen used to sing. The fact that the general public had only the final line to sing in each verse accounts for the low survival rate of Christmas songs dating from 400 or more years ago. Another difficulty was created by the use of Latin — sometimes in conjunction with German as in the celebrated: "In dulci jubilo, Now sing with hearts aglow".

Songs in earlier times

Other hymns were translations from the Latin. One that became very popular in Northern Germany and later in Protestant churches starts: "Quem pastores laudavere" – "Shepherds left their flocks astraying, God's command with joy obeying". That was translated at an early date, and its impact was heightened by being sung by two choirs, mostly boys voices. The first choir sang a Latin verse and the second choir came in with the German version. Boys choirs, singing for alms, existed in some parts of East Germany until after the Second World War. These boys, dressed in biretta and a dark cloak, went from house to house, street to street, singing Christmas songs for which they were rewarded with money.

They too mainly sang texts consisting of a mixture of German and Latin.

Songs since the Reformation

Hymns and Christmas songs received a great boost during the Reformation. For Protestants, the Roman-style mass no longer existed, and their Church services mainly consisted of proclamation of the Word of God and hymns. Martin Luther himself paved the way by translating a great many Latin hymns into German for congregational singing in church. Three of his Christmas songs are still popular today: "Vom Himmel hoch, da komm ich her", "Gelobet seist du, Jesus Christ", and "Vom Himmel kam der Engel Schar".

Luther did something very important in the first of these songs. He used the melody and also part of the text of a folk song. He certainly knew how much such a melody and text would appeal to believers. The folk song started with the words: "I come from far countries", and Luther changed that to: "From Heaven on high I come". Everyone would have immediately grasped what was involved. In the one case a traveller no-one knows comes from distant countries, and in the other an Angel, whom no-one may have seen before but is familiar from the Scriptures, comes down from Heaven. The reverse process can be observed today. Negroes in North American have been singing their moving spirituals at religious services since the 19th century — and all of a sudden one or other of these spirituals becomes a catchy folk song that is sung all over the place.

The first German hymn book — to which Luther contributed — appeared at Wittenberg in 1524. When the last such collection on which Luther worked appeared in 1545, a distinction was already being made between songs that should be sung and songs that might be sung on specific occasions. Other Reformation teachers took over Luther's approach, sometimes modifying it. Michael Weiße, a celebrated preacher belonging to the Moravian Brethren, became famous. These Brethren were the forerunners of the Moravian Church that has also established itself in North America. There is every justification for saying that these songs spread from Germany around the entire world. The followers of Calvin, for instance, took over the melodies from German hymn-books and composed French texts for them.

Highpoints of Church music

Luther's example also made a deep impression on Catholics. They saw how much singing fostered church services and could serve to strengthen a community. The first Catholic hymnal appeared in 1567, and there was no hesitation about including Protestant melodies and sometimes both music and words.

To begin with though, it continued to be the Protestant organists and choir-masters who always strove to produce new texts and melodies for the great annual festivals. They included Philipp Nicolai, who lived from 1556 to 1608. He wrote a number of Christmas songs — which are in fact more akin to Advent songs — including those starting: "How brightly beams the Morning Star", and "Awaken, calls the voice". His contemporary, Johann Heermann (1585—1647), was equally celebrated.

Then came the time of the Counter-Reformation when the Catholics attempted to regain the ground lost in the course of many wars and disputes. They had learnt from the Protestants the importance of hymns for services and the community. They had also perceived that respect for the Bible led Protestants to stick closely to the text involved, often failing to give expression to the feelings. The Catholics made up for that. A little community like Andernach on the Rhine in 1608 published its "Andernach Songbook" with text and melody for 187 songs. 46 of these are for Advent, Christmas, and Epiphany, and they include such celebrated songs as "There comes a ship a sailing" (Es kommt ein Schiff geladen) "An Angel came, bright and clear" (Es kam ein Engel hell und klar), and "There is a flower" (Es ist ein Ros' entsprungen). Those are songs that are always included when Christmas songs are sung in Germany.

Other German towns, no bigger than Andernach with its three to four thousand inhabitants, did likewise so that Andernach is only one example among many. People wanted to sing at Christmas, and they sang of their earthly lot and of the hope that had entered the world with the child in the crib.

Then followed the Baroque era with its many poets at courts and in towns, poets who wrote Christmas poems among other things and had these set to music. The song settings of Paul Gerhardt's "I stand by your crib" and Georg Weissel's "Open wide the door, Open wide the gates" became very well-known. Friedrich von Spee, a Jesuit Father, also wrote a number of Advent songs that are still popular, including "At Bethlehem is born a child to us" and "O Saviour, open up the heavens".

In the years that followed, there was not this wealth of expression and eloquent melody. Christmas songs were produced but are not so purely religious. The Enlightenment led people to turn away from faith and the ideas behind Christmas. The situation changed once again in the age of Romanticism when feeling for the meaning of religious songs was revived. It was then that Johann Daniel Falk wrote his "O du fröhliche, o du selige, gnadenbringende Weihnachtszeit" (O happy, o blessed Christmas) whose melody is said to be Sicilian in origin.

Ehre sey Gott in der Höhe
Friede auf Erden.

A. GABER.

Bild 34. Ehre sei Gott in der Höhe. 1855. Aus Beschauliches und
Erbauliches. Verlag Georg Wigand, Leipzig.

"Tower Music" (drawing by Ludwig Richter, 1855) at Christmas over a
hundred years ago . . .

. . . and in Frankfurt am Main today.

Silent night!
Holy night!
The most famous of all German Christmas songs, "Stille Nacht! heilige Nacht!", was also written at this time. Its history is extremely revealing since it demonstrates the speed with which such a song spread and, most importantly, its continuing popularity. The song was first heard during Christmas 1818 at the small church of St. Nicholas in Oberndorf, which is near Salzburg and the German-Austrian border. The writer of the text, Joseph Mohr, was assistant priest there from 1817 to 1819. Franz Xaver Gruber, the composer, had been the teacher and organist at nearby Arnsdorf since 1807, and he also filled the latter function at Oberndorf when no-one else was available. Just before Christmas 1818, Mohr suggested to Gruber that they should produce a new song for the festival. On the 24th of December he gave the musician his six verse text, thus leaving only a few hours till the moment when the song was due to be presented. The organist's melody pleased the poet though, and the song was performed at the Christmas mass to guitar accompaniment because the organ was in need of repair. The poet sang tenor, the composer bass, and the choir sang the last two lines in every verse. The man who repaired the organ told a group of Tyrolean singers about "Silent night", and they performed the song whilst touring Germany. It was first heard at Leipzig in 1831. Other Tyrolean groups took the song to the United States. It was sung at Hanover in 1840 and at Berlin shortly afterwards. "Silent night" was included in Protestant song-books at about the same time even though the writers of the text and the music had already been forgotten. It was long before their authorship was re-established. The song has now been translated into 44 other languages — and not just into such global tongues as English, French, Spanish, Portuguese, and Russian. That happened in less than a hundred years even though experts on music say that the melody is too sentimental, too sickly, and literary critics have still not accepted the text. It happened because between 1818 and the present day Christmas became a great festival throughout the world once non-Christian states got involved in the demands of diplomatic relations. Another contributory factor was the song's exceptional popularity in the United States. Many American soldiers who were in Europe during the First World War remembered little of their experience except the song about a silent, holy night:

Silent night! Holy night!
All is calm, all is bright,
Round yon Virgin Mother and Child.
Holy Infant, so tender and mild,
Sleep in heavenly peace,
Sleep in heavenly peace.

Silent night! Holy night!
Shepherds quake at the sight.
Glories stream from heaven afar,
Heav'nly hots sing "Alleluia,
Christ, the Saviour, is born,
Christ, the Saviour, is born."

Silent night! Holy night!
Son of God, love's pure light
Radiant beams from Thy holy face,
With the dawn of redeeming grace,
Jesus, Lord, at Thy birth,
Jesus, Lord, at Thy birth.

Christmas songs today

Christmas songs are written even today. It is not as if we only sing what was sung at Luther's time or around 1810. When the German youth movement flourished before the First World War, new songs were composed. That was also the case before the Second World War when the Churches and their festivals were at risk under the Nazis. The most famous of these writers was Jochen Klepper (1903—1942) with his "Night has fallen".
New Christmas songs are being produced constantly, inspired either by Alpine traditions or song-circles in the Catholic and Protestant Churches.

"Happy Christmas"

After the more serious Christmas songs, back again to something more light-hearted. "Tomorrow, children is the day" is full of joy and anticipation about the presents the Christ Child will leave under the tree for a good boy or girl. Very many dialect songs are even more joyous and exuberant. The Flemish and the Dutch sing of "The child in the stable", and people from the Alps sing of hosts of Angels somersaulting for joy from heaven down to earth. The Alpine areas are still a hive of activity since there are many groups of singers — as at the time of Mohr and Gruber — who want to extend their repertoire, which is partly in dialect and partly in High German.

Mention must again be made here of the miners, who have added their special contribution to Christmas for centuries. Their patron saint, Barbara, received homage on December the 4th, and then Christmas began for them. A special miners' Christmas song was recorded in the Erz mountains around 1830, showing that specific vocational groups celebrated the festivity in their own way. The first verse of this song runs:

> "Good luck, good luck!
> Miners rejoice, one and all!
> The Saviour of this mining world
> has his splendour unfurled.
> Hasten, miners, to serve him!
> Let no-one be left behind!
> Good luck, good luck, good luck!"

Handel, Bach, and Mozart

Christmas oratorios, classical masses, and concert arias take second place to these songs for Christmas. The composers involved include such names as Wolfgang Amadeus Mozart and George Frederic Handel whose "Rejoice, O Daughter of Zion" is often sung at Christmas. That almost exhausts the list. Christmas is a festivity for the family or a church community. Everyone participates in the spontaneous joy expressed in folk and church songs. Artistic oratorios and elaborate Christmas masses do not quite fit in there. Not even Johann Sebastian Bach's Christmas Oratorio exerts quite the attraction of his Passions. Anyone who wants to experience this antithesis should consider the contrast between the community celebrations in a big South German town like Munich and the rehearsed Mass, which, despite the marvellous music, remains — and must remain — an individual experience.

IX.

The Christmas Crib

"And she brought forth her firstborn son, and wrapped him in swaddling clothes, and laid him in a manger; because there was no room for them at the inn" (Luke 2,7). Ever since proclamation of the Gospel, this image has fascinated artists, major and minor, time and again.

Crib and cradle

This manger is the model for the Christmas crib. The word crib can also mean a basket — such as was used for a cradle. The Christmas crib, however, entails more than the Son of God's first earthly resting place. It involves the stable in Bethlehem and the animals, traditionally viewed as being between man and creation. It also involves the shepherds who came rushing from the fields when Angels told them of the birth of Christ. And it involves the Three Wise Kings from the East, guided by the star. The Christmas crib developed out of all these elements. Today it is very much in favour again throughout the Federal Republic. The retreat from the church into the family has been reversed, and cribs are again prominent in churches or even in museums.

A Christmas crib is thus a depiction of the birth of Christ as taken word by word from the Gospel. In this three-dimensional presentation, figures are shown in appropriate surroundings. They can be carved from wood — as is frequently done at present — or they can be made of clay or plaster of Paris and painted. Most of the figures in the smaller house cribs are somewhat stiff in appearance. That limits constructors of cribs to some extent. Most of the props for these little stages were made to last a long time so such cribs remain very similar over the years.

This "stage" can be either small, taking up little space, or it can be large. Some crib-lovers fill an entire room with their constructions. No matter what the scale, the scene centres around the birth, and German cribs usually present one of two possible settings. Firstly, there is the stable, which can be vividly evoked

Stable and cave

with the simplest of means. Great German painters such as Albrecht Dürer and Albrecht Altdorfer preferred this form of presentation with stars shining through the damaged roof of the semi-derelict building evoking the impoverished background to this event. The second possibility entails the cave in accordance with local tradition at Bethlehem. Mining communities used to take particular pleasure in making such cribs out of stiff sacking. In the middle of the stable or cave lies the infant Jesus, a tiny body that would not be noticeable among all the trimmings were it not for some bright clothing, a star overhead, or a halo. His mother kneels at his side. Her attitude of humility is a part of every characteristic crib. Tradition lays down that she wears a blue wrap or cloak over a red garment. Joseph is always an old man with a grey beard and inconspicuously dressed. He is scarcely mentioned in the Gospel so he remains an almost unnoticed figure in the background of the crib. Contemporaries have, however, often given him a little lantern, emitting the weak light of a tiny candle in realistic depictions, so as to boost his importance somewhat. The ox and the ass play a great part in such depictions though they are not even mentioned in the four Gospels (merely in a corrupt version of St. Mathew). Animals are part of a proper stable and attract young people's attention. That then is the indispensable core of any crib.

The shepherds   The shepherds constitute the second important group. "And they came with haste, and found Mary and Joseph, and the babe lying in a manger" — runs the Gospel. Makers of cribs have always endeavoured to capture the wonder and emotion precipitated by the Angel's message. The shepherds, men and women in simple and often poor clothes, hasten towards the manger. They carry crooks as tokens of their job, and often a bag for their provision. They approach the stable with an expression of wonder on their faces. The sheep have come along too, and are to be seen all around. In Italian villages, even today it is still the custom to bring the most recently born lamb to church for the service on Christmas morning. This scenario is often combined with a Christmas tree behind the crib so that the Angel (often with inscription) seems to hover in the tree.

The Wise Men   The Three Wise Men from the East constitute the third major group,
from the East   which is sometimes way in the background and sometimes not yet to be seen in Christmas Eve cribs. These Kings have always stimulated the imagination and creativity. Their clothing straight away stands out from that of the other groups. The Black King is exotically clad in robes similar to those still worn today by many African tribes. The two white Kings are also resplendently clothed, bringing gifts set in gold. Large cribs include servants and such

View of the "Christmas Mountain", Neustädtel, Erzgebirge.

unfamiliar animals as elephants, dromedaries, and camels. For our rural population, coming from scattered farms, villages, and little towns, this was the only opportunity each year for coming into contact with this outlandish world. No matter how imperfect such cribs may be, they impressively embody the text of the Gospel, contrasting the everyday and the dream. Outside there is winter with its cold, snow, rain, and early darkness — and inside the crib with its gold and mystery. It is hardly surprising that cribs are so popular with our young people!

Entire farm-houses with chickens and geese, even a small stream or pond with a bridge, are sometimes depicted. Ingeniously constructed fires burn on the fields of Bethlehem, and in the background there is the silhouette of an oriental town with lighted windows. There are little bushes and trees in the landscape, which is most convincingly created out of sand, moss, stones, roots, and painted backgrounds.

Cribs in churches   The cribs in churches are particularly large, and greater emphasis is again being put on such depictions of Christ's birth after many years of neglect. Many — and even older — churches have acquired the most recent of crib figures (usually carefully-dressed jointed dolls) which allow greater variety of use. They can stand in a different posture, with different clothes, every year. There are churches where parts of the Gospel story are presented as tableaux throughout the Christmas period. The cycle starts with the Annunciation, a popular and impressive scene with the Angel appearing to Mary. Next comes Mary's journey over the mountains to her cousin Elisabeth. Then follows the search for lodgings, a scene that has mainly become known through South German influences. The next scene is devoted to the birth, and that is succeeded by the adoration of the shepherds and Kings. Next is Jesus in the Temple, the circumcision, and finally the flight to Egypt. Models for all these scenes are provided by the most celebrated European sculptors and painters. Such presentations perhaps serve an educational function even more than a religious purpose. Most important of all though is a real joy in depiction of favourite scenes from the Bible.

Permanent cribs   There was another way of embodying the Christmas story for the faithful. This was incorporated in or even became the main feature of the altar around which the community held its daily service. We know the great carved altars in Southern Germany and Austria, and there are equally impressive creations on the other side of Germany along the Lower Rhine, in Flanders, and in the North Sea and Baltic areas. It would not be right to list the names of these carvers here. Their names are not always known anyway. Such work is exemplified though in the celebrated altars at Kalkar on the Lower Rhine, and in the splendid creations of the South German masters, headed by Tilman Riemenschneider. The church of St. Kastor at Karden on the Moselle is unique in having an Adoration of the Kings made from clay, which has survived on the High Altar for centuries despite the fragility of the material.

Varieties of crib   Such permanent representations have the disadvantage that they can never be changed. That is also the case with what are known

An 1830 "Christ Child", still completely baroque in style.

as box cribs presenting dioramas of the Christmas story. Such cribs used to be popular in Southern Germany, and were constructed by artists and sold to well-off families. They are very rare today and only to be found in museums. When mechanisation became fashionable around 1750, the technique was also applied to these cribs. A coin set the scene in motion. And what sights on which to feast the eyes! The shepherds and the Three Kings made their appearance. The animals moved. And even the Mother of God time and again raised her hands in praise.

These box cribs involved a highly attractive form of presentation. Boxes with different scenes from the Christmas story were assembled on a mini revolving stage. In scene one the stage was occupied by the Annunciation. For scene two there appeared the birth or the journey over the mountains. This form of crib was mainly cultivated from Upper Bavaria to Salzburg.

There is also a variant somewhat unfortunately known as the stage crib — where there is no stage. A cycle of paintings by Hans Memling on the birth of Christ (at the Pinakothek at Munich) depicts this as taking place in a town with its houses large and small, churches and palaces, and in the background roads leading over huge viaducts far into the countryside. Stage cribs are also dominated by architecture rather than landscapes. Even Matthias Grünewald's celebrated Isenheim Altar shows the Mother of God in surroundings characterised by buildings rather than scenery.

The Christmas Mount

What is called the Christmas Mount, which only existed in Saxony, constitutes a special form of crib. This can occasionally be found still, despite the destruction of many old religious customs during the war and post-war period that particularly affected this region. The Christmas Mount is a permanent crib varying in size. Some have even extended over half a room. There are the usual depictions of the birth, the Angel's appearance to the shepherds, the Three Kings, and a view of Bethlehem. The people who made these cribs lived in a mining area and were known as being skilled craftsmen so they added a characteristic feature of their home areas to such constructions. Singular happenings occurred both on and inside the mount. All the operations involved in mining were depicted. Ladders led down into the shafts and tunnels, and there were tiny wagons loaded with ore. Conveyor belts, moving the cage, went up and down. Miners, dressed for work, were to be seen everywhere — the man with the lantern, the hewer, and the boys loading and moving the wagons. Conveyor belts on wheels, powered by water, were known from the end of the 16th century, and this technique was preserved and improved by home-craftsmen among the miners. The Christmas Mount thus often

Clay crib from the Fichtelgebirge — fired and painted around 1850 by the Meyer family of potters from Marktredwitz.

contained a real little mine where miners' children could see for themselves how the work was organised. Little steam engines and electric motors were used at a later date to operate the complex mechanisms involved in such a Mount.

The origin of cribs   Why does the crib play such a part in Germany? From where do such depictions derive? What was the original intention? Indisputable written testimony exists stating that St. Francis of Assisi created the first such crib in a wood near Greccio in 1223. Painted, carved, and sculpted depictions of the birth of Christ had, of course, long existed. Old reference books report that the first depictions of the birth were to be found in the catacombs of Rome. St. Francis had something else in mind though. His intention was that this living presentation during a religious service should provide the faithful with embodiments increasing knowledge of the Gospel. He had a crib set up alongside the altar. This did not contain a child, and there was also no representation of the Mother of God and Joseph. The surroundings were developed in detail though with ox, ass, shepherds, and sheep. The Saint wanted his fellow-countrymen, simple people from the Italian mountains, to make the birth of Christ the focal element in their adorations. People came from far afield to experience this mass, and Francis preached a moving sermon on the child of Bethlehem. Legend reports that one of his friends was so touched that he had a vision of Christ in this crib. The Saint then took the child out of the cradle and embraced it.

The Franciscan order founded by St. Francis, the fratres minores, took up the idea of the crib. Their monasteries were mainly established in the towns of Europe as urban missions, and the crib was thus brought to these towns. The Dominicans, the other preaching order, also did much to spread this religious practice. The crib thus made its way from Italy through the Tyrol to Germany. It became well established in Westphalia, the Rhineland, and Upper Bavaria. Cribs were also to be found in Upper and Lower Franconia, Hesse, the Palatinate, Silesia, Saxony, and Pomerania, sometimes long after the Reformation since this popular form of Bible statement was much better understood than the abstract sermons of a trained theologians. The framework provided by the Gospel could be extended as desired and adapted to local circumstances. Despite this appeal to the population as a whole, the crib was largely restricted to churches for centuries. The church crib was also combined with long-established ceremonies, dances, and theatre, to which a separate chapter will be devoted.

Until 250 years ago, there were few exceptions to the rule that the crib as a representational depiction of the birth of Christ was the province of the church. In 1542 a certain Johann Brabender

Bavarian crib dating from the 19th century.

carved some moving, clothed figures for the cathedral clock at
Münster in Westphalia. The richly robed Three Kings and Mary
with her child still appear at noon every day right up to the present
whilst a glockenspiel plays "In dulci jubilo" and "Praise the Lord".

**The crib
in the family**

It was only around 1700 that cribs started appearing in family homes. That was partly an outcome of the Protestant Church wanting to have the theatricals and processions linked with the cribs banned from the House of God. About 80 years later, the Enlightenment also led more and more Catholics to want to remove what was regarded as a backward form of religiosity from the churches. These early home cribs were very simple. To begin with, it was often only Christ that was depicted as a baby in swaddling clothes. The head was modelled from wax, and the rest of the body consisted of a simple wooden shape covered with sumptuous material. The child was laid in a glass casket so as to prevent the wax melting or being knocked about. Wax was also used for the other figures that were gradually added to these cribs. There exist splendid examples of such figures in museums where they can be looked after and put on show. These wax cribs were made in at least the Rhineland and Westphalia until the mid 19th century — frequently by monasteries following Italian models. Poorer people turned to wood as a cheaper work-material, and their figures became more like familiar everyday characters than the models in church cribs. The shepherds, for instance, are 18th century Westphalian shepherds with their characteristic wooden shoes. The maid-servants have Westphalian-style bonnets and pack baskets. Unfortunately, only a few such local cribs still exist. More cribs have survived in Southern Germany, and these too give expression to local traditions. Such traditions survive better in remote mountain villages than in the urban areas of the Rhine and the Ruhr with constant fluctuations in the population.

There exists a very vivid description from the year 1863, recorded by O. von Reinsberg-Düringsfeld in Southern Germany. "The child rests in a dark grotto. Its mother kneels at the child's side, and Joseph stands at the entrance. Shepherds, mostly in mountain clothing, are kneeling before the cave or on the pasture where lambs are grazing and golden-winged Angels talking with other shepherds. One shepherd is generally depicted as rubbing the sleep out of his eyes, and in the foreground there is a spring where a cow is drinking. On the mountains, rising above the cave, there are houses and castles. Animals graze, protected by herdsmen, and huntsmen with rifles roam in search of hares and chamois. Horse and carts travel down the mountain-side, a butcher leads a calf, a farmer's wife brings eggs and butter, and a forester descends with a hare to be given to a child . . . The crib remains so until New Year when the circumcision is 'unveiled', followed on January the 5th by the Three Holy Kings. The Kings and their splendid retinue of pages, horsemen, and servants with horses, camels, and elephants fill the area in front of the crib, and this pomp provides the people's favourite presentation".

Pleasure in cribs began to decline around 1870. There were many causes. Factories started to supply mass-produced crib figures

Verre églomisé from Bavaria, end of the 18th century.

at relatively low prices, which led to a decline in personal involvement within the family. There was also a decline in religious conviction, and in Germany the state-church conflict following the 1870/72 Vatican Council. The Franco-Prussian War and other political changes exerted an influence too.

In 1892, Max Schmederer from Munich gave his private collection of cribs to the Bavarian National Museum, and this occupied over 1,000 sq. metres of exhibition space. This action led after the First World War to what was known as the crib movement. Well-known artists, priests, and writers established crib associations (for instance, The Association of Crib-Lovers in the Rhineland and Westphalia in 1925) so as to encourage the creation and exhibition of

The crib movement after 1900

"Straw crib" from the 1950s.

cribs in churches and homes once again. They were successful too. If you look for crib figures and materials before Christmas in Germany today, you will find a varied and artistically attractive range of products in the shops. Finally, mention should also be made of the "Krippana" at Heggersberg in the Eifel, the largest exhibition of church cribs in Europe.

Every year there are crib exhibitions at different places with the aim of showing people – particularly the young – how marvellously graphically and impressively the birth of Christ can be depicted even in our time.

X.

Christmas Performances

Processions were held in Houses of God to mark important church festivals even during the early phase of Christianity in Central Europe. People did not sit, as nowadays, at a fixed place in a church pew. There were usually no benches anyway, and the crowd was accustomed to pressing forward to the altar or to where the main focus of attention was during the service. At Easter, for instance, the Gospel text provided a number of roles. One person read the words of Christ and behaved as if he were Christ. Others took the parts of the accusers, Roman soldiers, Pontius Pilate, and the disciples. The faithful of the Middle Ages did the same with the Christmas story, presenting such scenes as the Angel Gabriel's appearance to Mary, and the conversation between the Three Kings and Herold in Jerusalem.

Beginnings in the Middle Ages

The child in the cradle remains the centre of all Christmas performances though. At the start of this long development, these performances may have been in Latin but people did at least have something to look at. That was limited in one respect, and a great deal in another. The less people understood, the more actively their imagination worked in order to make sense of what they saw. Under the influence of the Franciscans, who particularly venerated the Son of God and his Mother, the custom of performing plays with an established text spread rapidly through the church. From the 15th century onwards, they were also performed in German. There still exist copies of plays from Hesse and South Tyrol. It can also be assumed that these plays were spread throughout Germany before the Reformation. Such occasions were not always subdued and peaceful. Favourite excerpts from a number of plays were often performed so as to give as many people as possible something to say.

When these plays reached their climax, the child was taken out of the crib, and people started to dance and sing in its honour. The songs were a mixture of Latin and German such as the celebrated "In dulci jubilo, now sing with hearts aglow". The priests and monks did not always approve, maintaining that such goings-on infringed the dignity of a House of God and did not accord with a religious service. A town clerk from Hof an der Saale, close to the Fichtelgebirge, reported: "At Vespers on Christ's Holy Day, the Child Jesus was cradled in accordance with the old custom. The organist played "Resonet in laudibus — Joseph, dearest Joseph mine, help me cradle the child divine", and the choir sang this, and almost turned such songs into a dance. Then young men and women in the church used to start dancing around the altar, and that was called the Pomwitzel Dance . . .". During these scenes, a previously chosen girl or some other people took the little body depicting Jesus from the crib, and cradled this in time with the music. After — or even during the service — the crib and child stood on the altar. This custom was known throughout Germany as cradling the child.

"Bornkinnel" This joyous and sometimes uncouth celebration was gradually driven out of the church into the portals or onto the church steps, which contributed to transfer of the crib to individual homes. More recent reports from Saxony and the Rhineland demonstrate though that this custom kept a footing in the church. Despite all the efforts of Protestant preachers, the Christ Child could not be forced out of churches in Saxony. This embodiment bore the remarkable name of "Bornkinnel", which is variously translated as the child born to us or the child that is cradled. In areas where the Saxon dialect is spoken today though, the name signifies a present marking Christmas and joy in the festival. In some Saxon communities, it was still customary after the Second World War to include a kind of dumb show during the service. Pastors mainly did that to open young people's eyes to the Gospel.

The child was cradled during the Christmas service at Blankenberg an der Sieg, a little town in the Rhineland, until recent times. This was similar to what was recorded by the chronicler of Hof. The organ played a song whose rhythm set off a cradle-like movement among all those attending church. "Everyone stayed put at the end of the service until the three parts and their repetitions had been played once again, and the Christ Child had thus been cradled" — according to a school chronicle. Today the organist no longer knows this difficult melody, and churchgoers are also shy about joining in this cradling movement.

Christmas processions That was not, however, the end of the Christmas play. It may have been taken over by laymen but it has been preserved up to the present day. People needed something to look at, and they found it here. The custom of presenting the birth of Christ in a theatrical form has survived best in the German Alps. It was also the custom in Franconia for a small troupe of well-rehearsed players to give such performances at various places in the days after Christmas. Roles were distributed and scenes worked up so as to provide the public with the essence of any theatrical performance — joy, sadness, fear, and emotion.

These performances were made even more attractive by concluding them with a distribution of presents for children. The Christ Child handed over the presents the parents had previously bought or made. In some places this distribution of presents is all that has survived of what had once been a flourishing Christmas play. In the north of the Palatinate and the Hunsrück, a Christ Child still goes from house to house to take presents to families with small children. A girl of 13 or 14 usually takes this part, dressed in white clothing and a veil. She is accompanied by other girls representing Angels.

The crib play resurrected (Salzburg)

This link between live presentations and the crib is important. The custom of setting up a crib under the family Christmas tree would never have established itself if this representation had not served as a substitute for such performances. It was the custom in mining towns in Upper Silesia to display self-made cribs on January the 6th, Epiphany. The Three Kings and their retinue made their way through the villages. After the First World War, people all over the world started to reflect on the extent to which man had got embroiled in technology and power politics, and there was a fresh blossoming of the crib and the play around the crib. Celebrated poets and artists created plays, and some of these were also enthusiastically received in the theatre. After the Second World War, this movement arose again, and between 25,000 and 30,000 visitors from all over the world come to Salzburg every year to experience the Advent Singing in the great Festival Hall. On the stage that during the summer is devoted to operas by Mozart, Beethoven, and Verdi with the world's best singers, ordinary people from the mountain areas roundabout present the story of the birth of Christ. Recitation combined with music and song put across the meaning of this season of year. When such an evening ends with everyone on the stage and in the hall singing "Silent Night", you know that this tradition still lives.

Lay performances

The tradition of the Christmas play is not completely at an end either even where the resources of a Salzburg are lacking. The time from Christmas to Twelfth Night favours family celebrations, meetings between friends, and paying visits. It has also long been customary for clubs and organisations to hold their annual meetings and elections at this time. Such occasions are often accompanied by amateur theatricals. Groups are still active here and there even though television may have very much undermined initiative and involvement. These lay groups seldom present plays about the birth of Christ any longer. They mainly perform serious plays, intended to lead people to do good works.

Christmas in the theatre Urban theatres and court ensembles in the 18th and 19th centuries also took note of the public's readiness to go to the theatre at this time of year. It was as if they had to perform plays for children around Christmas. They realised that good money was to be earned in this way — principally because the self-respecting middle classes wanted to take their children to the theatre at Christmas. Such performances started in cities like Berlin and Hamburg in the 1780s and 1790s. This was often a case of needs-must-be for travelling players who otherwise had no chance of earning anything during these "quiet" days. Initially they performed pieces with some relevance for the festival. Splendid scenes could be made of the journey of the Three Wise Men from the East to Jerusalem and on to Bethlehem. Then the players devised material that could be combined with Christmas celebrations. The links with religion largely vanished though, and the emphasis changed to adapting fairy tales and legends for the stage. Little or nothing remained of Christmas.

This fashion came to an end round about 1960. Television offered strong competition, and the stories were so sentimental and unconvincing that parents no longer let their children go to such performances. Here and there a theatre still thinks it has to put on a fairy tale on Boxing Day but the effort is wasted.

XI.

The Three Kings and Their Star

The customs surrounding Epiphany have come to the fore again after having lost ground throughout Europe in recent decades. In the countries of Christendom, it took centuries before the festival of Christmas prevailed over Epiphany. The Day of the Three Kings was originally viewed as being of greater importance than the day of Christ's birth. The Church formerly thought that Jesus was first recognised as the Son of God in the adoration of the Magi at the crib in Bethlehem. The young Church therefore set the baptism in the Jordan as having taken place on January the 6th as part of the symbolism of correspondences between Christ's life and time of year. For a Christian, life only begins with baptism rather than with the actual birth. The miracle of the star provided clear-cut testimony to Christ's special standing in the world order. No mortal had ever been accorded such an extra-terrestrial honour. The new year thus started with the festival of the Three Kings or the Three Wise Men from the East — and the Orthodox Church still adheres to that. This day thus became one of the year's most important festivals. It was also the thirteenth day after the birth of Our Lord. All Epiphany carols refer to the fact that the Wise Men must have travelled a great distance in the course of these thirteen days.

Epiphany

This festival became of great significance for Germany when in the year 1164 Emperor Friedrich Barbarossa gave permission to Rainald von Dassel to take the remains of the Three Wise Men as spoils of war from Milan, newly captured, back to his cathedral city of Cologne. Cologne thus came into possession of one of the most venerable graves in Christianity. No grave existed of the Mother of God, and the location of St. Joseph's was unknown. The masters of Cologne Cathedral decided to extend the building into what became a world-famous edifice, and they called in the most skilled of goldsmiths to create the Shrine of the Three Kings. Throughout the Middle Ages, a pilgrimage to Cologne was one of Christianity's great experiences, almost as important as a journey to the Holy Land or to Santiago de Compostela in Spain.

Cologne Cathedral and the Shrine of the Three Kings

Veneration of these saints spread from Cologne to Flanders and the Netherlands, to Hildesheim and Westphalia, to Silesia, to East Prussia and Poland, to the Danube area, Hungary and Romania, and also to Switzerland through which the precious relic had been transported from Milan. This veneration left traces everywhere, particularly in the form of popular plays about the Three Kings based on biblical sources as embellished over the centuries.

Epiphany customs These plays were probably performed wherever the Three Kings were venerated. There must have been many such plays, none of which have survived to the present day. One element has, however, been preserved or revived. This is known as Star-Singing, and consists of three people, embodying Caspar, Melchior, and Balthasar, and their retinue, going from house to house through villages and towns during Epiphany. They receive a gift at each house. In earlier times these gifts were divided between the Three Kings, which is why this Star-Singing was frowned on and condemned by the Church and the authorities in the 19th century. There are tales about how these groups sang their way around without any sign of the original religious significance. The proud procession of Kings, retinue, and presents for Jesus thus degenerated into a group of scroungers, and that is why the custom gradually faded away in Germany except for Danzig and Upper Silesia (till the 1930s) and isolated areas of the Rhineland, Belgium, and Luxemburg. Carl Hauptmann, Gerhart's less-celebrated brother, provides vivid descriptions in his work of the great impression made by this Star-Singing during his youth in the Riesengebirge around 1870.

The Star The star was the focal point of these processions, and the star and the Black King were the greatest attractions. Around 1789 the star in Thuringia — and elsewhere too — was described as follows: "The star consists of a pole to which is attached a board. On this board there stands (in the background) a kind of castle made of cardboard, richly decorated with gold and box-wood. On the one side are box bushes where the Three Kings are concealed until the song demands their appearance — and on the other is the stable with Joseph, Mary, and the child in the crib together with an ox and a donkey. At the centre of the castle there is a large window behind which stands Herod, usually with a terrible reddish-brown face adorned with a wig. All these figures are on strings, and are moved when the text demands this by the Kings posted on both sides. A large, gilded, cardboard star, filled with peas, is fixed to the rod, and revolved by the star-bearer. Everything is illuminated by three or four small lights".

One line in the song sung on this occasion has become well-known, and runs: "A poor king am I, Pass me not uncaring by".

W.WERTHMANN.SC.

Die heiligen drei Könige mit ihrem Stern,
sie essen, sie trinken und zahlen nicht gern.

"Three Kings Song" by Ludwig Richter, 1855.

Children throughout the Rhineland, in Bremen, and elsewhere have taken over those very lines and incorporated them in a song used when they go from house to house, seeking gifts, on St. Martin's Day.

Star-Singing   This custom of Star-Singing experienced a revival after the Second World War. The heads of Catholic missionary organisations in all German-speaking areas — the Federal Republic of Germany, Austria, Switzerland, Eastern Belgium, Luxemburg, and Alsace — realised that this traditional custom could be employed for a new purpose. That led to the great Star-Singing movement, which still prevails throughout these areas. On the Sunday closest to Epiphany a troupe of young singers assembles in front of the church door, and sing Epiphany carols to the accompaniment of guitars and other instruments. The parts of the Three Kings are usually taken by three boys, about fourteen years old, arrayed in exotic garments. They wear golden crowns made from cardboard, and the Black King bears the golden star. They no longer collect biscuits, dried fruit, and other things to eat. They collect money in the jewel caskets they are holding. Such collections take place all over the country, and the proceeds are devoted to missionary activities in Third World countries.

These troupes often wander for days from farm to farm in remote areas of Bavaria, Westphalia, Lower Germany, and through the many villages of the Mittelgebirge so as gather as much money as possible. There is real competition to see who gets most money for this good cause, and millions of DM are collected. All the farmhouses in Southern Germany, no matter how remote, place great importance on being visited by such groups of singers. Without the star-singers they risk misfortune. Most of these songs are completely new with catchy tunes and there are also regional variations. The first lines of such songs demonstrate that themes and references have remained the same despite the passing of time. One starts: "Gaze on the star we bring from afar, a star of heavenly splendour". The star is therefore still very important, which is why inventive people fit electric lights into stars and get them to rotate. Another song begins: "We come from the East, led by God's hand" — and people from mountain areas of the South enjoy singing "From afar we come to praise, four hundred miles in thirteen days".

Our days have brought an important change in this custom — and coaxed an amused smile out of many a spectator. In this age of equality of the sexes, almost as many girls as boys — if not a greater number — now take part. There is, however, as yet no record of girls being dressed up as the Kings because they do not like being "made black" to represent the Moorish Monarch.

Wrought-iron work, depicting the Three Kings, at an inn in Biberach
an der Riß (South Germany).

Scholarship has, by the way, established that all three kings were depicted as being white until around 1400. Only from that time onwards did painters and artists portray the youngest king, Caspar, as being black.

Blessing the home   There is another custom that falls at Epiphany, mainly in Silesia and around the Alps. The pastor goes the rounds of his parish to bless homes. He is accompanied by two ministrants, one with holy water and the aspergillum, and the other with a censer, which is swung to and fro, emitting a sweet aroma. When the priest enters a house, he first blesses the family by making the sign of the cross with holy water. He then prays for peace and security in the house, and writes the letters "C + M + B" and the year on the door, beam, or posts. The reader will have guessed that the letters stand for the names of the Three Kings. Their intercession will hold good for anyone who enters or leaves the consecrated house. In earlier times, the full names were written on the door, and a small cross was included between them so that the house was really blessed and protected. The same idea is involved when Jews attach a scroll containing the Pentateuch and the ten commandments to the door or house posts. In Alpine valleys and other remote places, the father of the family writes the three letters and the cross on the door, and then the youngest son carries the incense censer through the house and the stable. This is intended to drive evil out of the homestead. There was a deeper meaning behind this too. Each of the Three Kings had a specific task. Caspar, the bearer of gold, had to pray that the house did not lack its daily bread. Melchior, the King of Light (incense), had to ensure that the fir never went out. If it was extinguished, so too was human life. Balthasar, who brought myrrh, guaranteed God's protection. The Church may have desired to undermine this custom's associations with superstition when it reinterpreted the three letters as "Christus mansionem benedicat" (Christ bless this house). In this form, the custom made its way to the West by way of millions of refugees and expellees from Germany's former eastern provinces after the Second World War. It found unusually rapid acceptance and recognition among much of the population. Doors marked in this way are even to be found in cities. Anyone who knows how heterogeneous our cities are with the religious and the non-religious, the pious and declared atheists, living alongside one another will realise the implications for a custom whose origins were ultimately religious.

Significance of this festival   There is more to be said about the customs associated with this day but that belongs elsewhere in this book. One aspect of Epiphany must be stressed though — at least with regard to the Federal Republic of Germany. The decline in such customs now taking place shows how much the Christmas period has gained

"Adoration of the Kings" by Albrecht Dürer, 1504. The King in the middle is probably a self-portrait of the artist.

in importance over the past century. The former rivalry between Christmas and Epiphany has been decisively resolved in favour of the festival of Christmas. How quickly the significance of Epiphany has dwindled since about 1920! That receives expression in deletion of this day from the list of official public holidays in most of Germany's federal states. The Church celebration has also been put back to the following Sunday. Even in Cologne, the saints' resting-place, the 6th of January is the same as any other work-day except for the fact that a high mass, incomparable in its festive splendour, is celebrated in the cathedral that morning. The Emperor's bell, the largest German bell, is sounded at the start of this service. This is so heavy that 28 men were needed to get it going before introduction of an electric mechanism. This bell is heard very seldom — at Christmas, Epiphany, Easter, Whitsun, and Corpus Christi — since the cathedral architect fears for the safety of the bell tower.

One other aspect of Epiphany is worthy of mention. In homes where there are children and a crib, the father or mother secretly adds the figures of the Three Kings and their retinue to the crib display on the morning of January the 6th. The children are delighted when they become aware of this. The same happens in churches where the cribs thus attain to artistic completion in more than one sense.

XII.

Ancient Beliefs from Advent to Epiphany

A German poet whose name is not even known provides the earliest use (1190) of the designation 'Hallowed Night':

Hallowed Night and Christ's Night

"He is mighty and strong,
The man who was born in the Hallowed Night.
He is the Holy Christ".

Thus begins a verse by this minstrel. The use of 'Hallowed Night' raises problems. Normal usage at that time would have been 'Holy Night' or 'Christ's Night', but the poet employed a term that dates further back. This Germanic term cannot be Christian in origin. The Germanic peoples' winter solstice and the Christian Holy Night fell on the same day, but it was at the relatively late date of 354 A.D. that the Church decreed the birth of Christ should be celebrated on December the 25th.

It was not just the Germanic peoples though who celebrated the day of the invincible Sun God. The Romans also marked the day when the God started to direct his chariot northwards again, and the days became longer. On that depended the date laid down for the start of the New Year, which was different in the old Julian calendar to today's Gregorian system. When the latter was introduced in 1582, ten days had to be made good. A Papal decree stated that the 5th of October 1582 should be followed by the 15th of October. The Reformation had, however, long since swept through Europe, and Protestant states were not ready to accept Rome's decision just like that. England only introduced the new calendar in 1752, extensive areas of Germany in 1776, and Russia as late as 1918.

Today's dates

The well-known differences in important dates around Christmas result from that. In all the Eastern churches, the 6th of January, Epiphany, is still viewed as the most important day in this festive season, uniting the adoration of the Three Kings and the start of the New Year. All German Protestants from what is now the GDR and Poland still of one accord refer to "The High New Year" instead of Epiphany. The actual New Year's Day would be of little significance for Christians were it not for the festivity on the previous day named after Pope Silvester I. The Day of Lights, the 13th of December, constituted a very important date according to the old calendar but today it is only a Nordic festival. All that remains in Germany is a bit of country lore about the days becoming longer after the Day of Lights. Under the Julian calendar, December the 13th entailed the longest night and the shortest day. That now happens on Thomas's Day, the 21st of December.

Advent   Advent's position between the old and the new years makes this season something special right up to the present day. The churches see it as the start of the new church year whereas in secular terms Advent Sunday signals the final weeks of the old year. For the Catholic Church, Advent was for many centuries a time for repentance and fasting. The church liturgy was directed towards something still to happen in the future so it is not surprising that many events were endowed with a significance extending beyond the immediate moment. St. Nicholas's attendant was originally there to drive away evil. Masked figures performed this function in Southern Germany by rampaging through the villages so as to chase away demons wishing to establish themselves in this dark time. Other companions, totally enveloped in straw, served the same function. Such figures were even better established in Northern Germany — particularly Pomerania and East Prussia — where they rule alone without St. Nicholas. Terrifying figures of a man on a withe horse, a stork, and witches, all embodied by people, were intended to drive out terror and fear of darkness. All these antagonists were emanations of the superstition in which this time of year is so rich. In the Erzgebirge on the fourth Sunday in Advent, people went so far as to put out lights and food in hallways in order to keep evil spirits from entering the house itself.

In Switzerland, Austria, and Bavaria, young men went from house to house, knocking on the shutters and doors, on the last three Thursdays in Advent. Here again the object was to drive away evil. The nuts, grains, peas, and beans that rained into rooms when the Julklapp came served the same purpose.

Christmas Night   These superstitious ideas reach a climax in Christmas Night. The night in which Christ was born must, after all, be a night full of wonders. Animals can speak then, and anyone who has the gift and does what is necessary can understand them. Rare plants grow in the snow and ice for this one night, and then vanish again for the rest of the year. Water can become wine. The fire in the hearth will last throughout the year if a special slow-burning log is used — as a few people still believe in Westphalia. As already mentioned, the green of the fir tree, box, holly, yew, and juniper is symbolic of life, and intended to help overcome night, death, and infertility. It is not all that long ago that people used to invoke trees and fruit bushes in this Christmas Night to contemplate the blossoming to come.

Even today, people have not been able to completely free themselves from the magic of this night. Quite the contrary in fact, if you look at many Christmas stories and poems where there are frequent references to miraculous events and encounters which man should not shun. He should also remain open to the unhoped for encounter with a hitherto unknown fellow being, who can be a vehicle for the miraculous.

The Twelve Nights

The Holy Twelve Nights, which last until the night of 5/6 January, start with Christmas Night. They have various names. In South Germany it was the custom to burn incense against evil spirits. In Eastern Bavaria and the area around Salzburg, father and son still go throughout the house with a censer on the Holy Night. This censer contains glowing coals onto which resin is scattered so as to disseminate a powerful fragrance. Belief in the Twelve Nights is also still strong in the Altmark to the East of the Elbe in North Germany. These nights contain many dangers. Even today people throughout Germany avoid doing any washing during this time — except for babies' needs. Anything except absolutely necessary washing brings misfortune. White washing hanging on the line is thought to indicate a coffin in the family, laid out with such linen. Work that is not completely unavoidable also brings ill luck. Threshing was strictly avoided at this time of year. There was also a prohibition on using a spinning wheel or sewing machine. This is a tranquil time that should not be disturbed.

The Twelve Days

Each of these twelve days contains important foreshadowings of the twelve months in the year ahead. The first day provides revelations about January, the second about February, and so on. All natural phenomena — snow and rain, freeze and thaw, clouds, rises in temperature, and possibly even winter thunder — were closely observed and as far as possible interpreted. Much rural lore about the weather dates from this time.

Dreams at this time of year were scrutinised with particular intensity. Dreams during these Twelve Nights were thought to be especially revelatory. "What a man dreams between Christmas and New Year is fulfilled". The Bible is much referred to in this context. An Angel twice appeared to Joseph in a dream, and called on him to take action that turned out to be beneficial. The message in a dream does not have to be pleasant though. "If a man lies on a bier during these Twelve Days, someone from the village will die each month throughout the year".

Auguries on New Year's Eve

New Year's Night marks the high-point of this time for looking into the future. This starts with casting lead towards midnight. This lead oracle is particularly productive for marriageable young women since the hissing lumps of lead thrown into cold water often provide indications of the job and name of the husband-to-be. The lead's powers of prediction are even greater if the lumps of metal are held in front of a candle and the shadow thrown on the wall studied in detail. In the region between the rivers Sieg and Wupper, girls used to gaze into the flickering firelight and espy the face of the man they were to marry. If the first person you met on New Year's Day was an old woman, you would be out of luck for that day and possibly for the entire year. A black cat is equally feared. The chimney sweep is supposed to bring luck though. In big cities like Berlin and Hamburg, you could hire a chimney sweep for group photos since they were not to be seen at work on a public holiday.

Men throughout Germany like going to a pub and playing cards on New Year's Eve. They want to try their luck. They used to play for pretzels, which were very popular at New Year. Oatmeal biscuits covered with the local pear or apple spread were much appreciated too. The clear-cut favourite for New Year's Eve in North Germany today is sausages with potato salad whereas people in the Rhineland prefer a hering salad (see Recipes).

Back to the auguries though. In Silesia it was customary for marriageable girls to lie on the floor at midnight and throw a shoe backwards over their heads. The toe of the shoe then pointed towards the direction from which the future bridegroom would come.

Dice are employed elsewhere in a game of fortune on the last day of the old year. This is to be found along the Rhine, in the Ruhr, and in parts of Westphalia where people in pubs and cafés throw dice for cakes, ham sandwiches, and other edibles. In Upper Silesia there used to be a custom that was carried out on Christmas Eve but directed towards the New Year. A scale was taken from the traditional Christmas carp for each person seated around the table. This was put under each plate together with a coin so as to ensure that happiness and money lasted throughout the year. In East Prussia there were even oracular games. In one of these, "Grasp your fortune", New Year biscuits hinted at the entire scala of human destiny with depictions of a man, a woman, a ring, a doll, a cradle, a ladder, a stone, and a skull. The players have their eyes blindfolded, and must then take three biscuits. If, for instance, they get three dolls, that signifies a child in the year ahead. Attention must be paid during this night to a thousand and one details that cannot be enumerated here.

New Year's Eve is also a time — perhaps even more so than Christmas — for giving pleasure to other people. Young people in the Sauerland, Bergisches Land, and the Westerwald used to go from house to house, singing a multi-part song. When the song was over, guns were fired and the troupe's leader chalked the new date on house doors. People in the houses expressed their recognition in the form of money or agricultural produce so that the young men could stay together afterwards in the pub. Anyone who did not do that was mocked as being stingy, a greedy donkey. A donkey was also drawn on his door instead of the date. In the villages and towns of Altmark, New Year's processions have scarcely changed up to the present day. Places with a reputation to maintain have brass music performed from the church tower on New Year's Eve. This is usually a religious melody but the tune at Lüdenscheid in Westphalia was "The old year is past". Old drawings show that the custom of singing and music-making used to exist throughout Germany. In places where this custom declined, specific individuals were engaged to take over this function. In many places, the night watchman had the task on New Year's Eve of blowing a beautiful song as well as sounding the hours on his horn — for which he was suitably rewarded. This custom has experienced a great revival wherever brass-players are to be found since people find the practice beautiful and meaningful. Distribution of New Year's presents is still a custom throughout Germany too. The main beneficiaries are people who serve the public year-in year-out such as postmen, dustmen, servants, long-service employees, security guards, etc.

Omnipresent and most important of all though is the noise with which the old year is driven away on the stroke of midnight. This custom extends from the Alps to the North Sea, from the big cities to the smallest hamlet. In the Alps, the local riflemen's association takes care of that, and elsewhere it is young unmarried men. In towns, individual families chase off the old year with rockets, gun salutes, shouts, and noise in general. Every year, newspapers tell their readers how many million DM worth of fireworks were shot off to mark the New Year. As early as 1711, the Prince of Hesse promulgated an edict against this "foolish" custom — but to little effect even though it was repeated from time to time.

Driving out the old year

At midnight all the church bells are rung. Telephones are busy with relatives and friends ringing from all over the place so as to gain the secret advantage entailed in conveying New Year greetings. Even in the intimate circle of the family, the fixed custom is to wish everyone present a "Happy New Year" ("Prosit Neujahr"). This greeting should also be conveyed to any remaining friends and relations on New Year's Day. Older people like the younger generation to take the initiative here. Children go to their god-parents in the morning to wish them the best for the New Year, and usually get some money in return.

Drinks on New Year's Eve are also meant to serve good fortune in the New Year, and these are often enjoyed in considerable quantities. Sparkling wine and punch are the favourites. Mulled wine — usually made from red wine, lemons, sugar, cinnamon, and cloves — is also popular. In Thuringia and elsewhere in Central Germany, fish is eaten on New Year's Eve.

The tradition of the New Year's Eve ball, often bringing together hundreds of people, comes from the upper middle classes. The first carnival gatherings often take place then in the Rhineland, Baden, and the Black Forest. The New Year celebrations thus introduce the good cheer of dancing, music, and cabaret-like entertainment into the basically serious time of Advent and Christmas. In ninety nine cases out of a hundred, festival performances at the theatre are devoted to Johann Strauß's operetta "Die Fledermaus".

Twelfth Night The 6th of January, Epiphany, is another important day. Balls are also held on this day, and it is the custom in the Rhineland to discover the Bean King and the Bean Queen. Two beans are included in the doughnuts baked to mark this festive occasion. Popular belief has it that one of the beans will be found by an unmarried man and the other by an unmarried woman, and the two will become husband and wife. This custom came from England and very quickly established itself in the Rhineland, Westphalia, Berlin, and East Prussia. At private gatherings, the Bean King and the Bean Queen take over responsibility for keeping the party going. This custom dates back to the Middle Ages when the King also had to fulfil specific religious functions.

As already mentioned, Epiphany includes elements of heathen and pre-Christian customs. Here as elsewhere it becomes apparent how skilfully church festivities made use of existing traditions. In Southern Bavaria people still talk about "Berchta's Day" in memory of Lady Berchta, a Goddess in the Germanic and Rhaeto-Romanic pantheon. "Mother Holda" was ceremoniously burnt on this day at Eichsfeld, now close to the GDR border. You are supposed to eat particularly well on the Day of the Three Kings so that the evil spirits' knives slip off your bursting stomach. Divin-

"Christmas" by Daniel Chodowiecki (1799) who has a high reputation as "visual chronicler" of 18th century Berlin.

ing rods are particularly good if they are cut on this day since their users will be able to find gold, silver, and water in the name of the Kings. Epiphany missives, printed in Cologne and brought in contact with the Shrine of the Three Kings, are thought to provide protection against hail and lightning. In Upper Silesia, a procession of Epiphany singers complete with goblins and bears, making clear the originally pre-Christian nature of the ceremony, made its way through the villages.

The Twelve Days and Nights come to an end with Epiphany. The days get visibly longer, and the darkness gradually yields. The light has gained the upper hand again by Candlemas on February the 2nd. The last Christmas trees, which are usually taken out of the house on the Day of the Three Kings, are put out in the garden or on a rubbish tip. Carnival is close at hand.

Such superstitions may seem strange to some readers. "Things like that don't happen any more. Those times are over for good" — say some people. Anyone though who has looked into the background to Christian customs can say without exaggeration that such ideas and belief in forces beyond science and theology have not vanished. They are very much alive among us — as is sufficiently demonstrated in survivals of popular folklore and by a glance at the horoscopes in newspapers and magazines, resort by many people to the fortune-teller, and table-turning and all the rest of spiritualism.

Christmas pyramid from the Erzgebirge (photo from the early 20th century).

123

XIII.

Eating and Drinking at Christmas
by Ulrich Tolksdorf

As a succession of several traditional feast days — starting, perhaps, with St. Martin's Day (November the 11th), and then carrying on with St. Catherine's Day (November the 25th), St. Nicholas' Day (December the 6th), the four Advent Sundays, Christmas Eve, Christmas and Boxing Days, New Year's Eve and Day, up to Epiphany (January the 6th) — the Christmas season, like any festivity, has since time immemorial also been an occasion for considerable eating and drinking. Eating and drinking, inclusive of all the goodies baked for Christmas, constitute a genuinely traditional element. In North Germany, for instance, Christmas Eve is known as "Full Belly Eve" or "Fat Belly Eve" — and Christmas is not a leisurely or contemplative time for doctors today since there is no other time of year when they have so many patients with stomach upsets.

General considerations

Today's succumbing to the culinary delights of Christmas was paralleled in the popular beliefs of former times. "Anyone who eats much on Christmas Eve will be well-off throughout the year" — or "Anyone who gets up hungry from the Christmas table will suffer hunger for the next year". This is not just a matter of popular superstition though. Religious and economic reasons played a part too. In the old days, Christmas brought to an end a period of strict fasting for Advent with the result that attention was naturally directed towards worldly pleasures once again. On the other hand, the great dependence of farming and general consumption patterns on seasonal rhythms of activity made the Christmas period seem particularly suitable for celebrations. Spring was always a "time of shortages" and "pre-harvest hunger" was the norm, and late autumn was a "time of abundance" when the harvest was brought in and the Central European climate permitted a rest from work on the land.

People in the Federal Republic of Germany today probably know little about the historical antecedents of Christmas baking, boiling, and roasting. All the same, every house is pervaded year in year out with the aroma of Christmas baking weeks before the festival.

There has been no decline in pleasure in baking for Christmas — despite the increased range of commercial products available. Even housewives who do not otherwise like cooking or have their hands full elsewhere take time to bake for their families. This Christmas baking is very much encouraged by children who help decide what should be cooked and how it should be decorated.

Many of today's Christmas cookies and dishes in the Federal Republic date back a long way, and their form, preparation, and symbolic significance can often be traced back to the 13th century. That is particularly true of Christmas biscuits. In earlier times, it was mainly the monasteries that devoted themselves to such biscuits, and brought special products onto the market for the established Church festivals.

Even today though, scholars are still not completely agreed on the origin and function of certain forms of biscuit and associated beliefs over the centuries. They demonstrate Christian reinterpretation of sacrificial, death cult, and fertility aspects of ancient Germanic mythology. It would, however, be going too far in this context to discuss individual instances of the way in which such transmissions have occured. Suffice it to say that the forms and ideas of centuries long past live on in Christmas biscuits in different parts of **Germany**.

Baking for the festivity The great diversity of Christmas confectionary in Germany almost exceeds comprehension, and foreigners visiting the Federal Republic are constantly amazed. There used to be some special kind of baker's ware for every festivity throughout the year or a person's life. The shape and preparation of these wares for special occasions varied greatly from town to town, or at least from region to region. This tradition still existed at the start of the century. Aspects of these old customs have certainly been lost since then, and technical progress has produced changes in both home and commercial baking. That has led to a degree of unification in recipes and Christmas biscuits. Another decisive change took place after 1945. The influx of refugees and expellees combined with greater general mobility resulted in a diversity of Christmas confectionary becoming available almost everywhere in the Federal Republic — as compared with only one or two generations ago when only local and traditional forms were to be found in a locality.

This diversity of characteristic regional Christmas confectionary with all its links with a multiplicity of popular beliefs and customs is so great that only selected examples can be presented here. A modest collection of recipes is intended to provide an incentive towards baking for yourself.

The rich treasury of forms and the traditional concepts involved in Christmas baking are best demonstrated in the bread and biscuits baked in special shapes, depicting human beings, saints, fairy-tale and traditional figures, animals, parts of the body, stars, and various abstract symbols. In earlier cultures, they had some cultic or sacrificial significance, and were linked with fertility rites or oracular activities. Such special shapes are known among many peoples almost all over the world, and originally involved sacrifices of food by peasant cultures. Most of these wares certainly date back very far, but there are also new creations which are meant to invoke old symbols. Reutlingen's New Year cookie is reminiscent of but different to the Germanic solar disc, and was specially created for the town's Shooting Festival by a master baker with a keen nose for business. "Wreaths" or "Rings" are otherwise usual almost everywhere in Germany, and these are popularly interpreted even today as meaning that the year has completed its course. In East Prussia, the game known as "Grasp your fortune" used to involve New Year biscuits. The players were blind folded, and had to make three choices from a variety of pastry figures — a woman, man, ring, cradle, doll, key, ladder, stone. skull, etc. If a similar figure was taken three times, the event symbolised was expected to come to pass.

Animal figures (Horse, wild boar, pig, goat, stag, hare, cock, and hen sitting on eggs) are the most popular figures even today. In former cultures they served as sacrifices but now the emphasis is playful and joking. Even today some children choose their "domestic pet" or "woodland creatures" for such baking, and hang these pastries on fruit trees or bushes. That still frequently happens at the New Year when old oracles and invocation of the year ahead are in full swing, even if only in fun.

Depictions of heavenly bodies (Moon, crescent, stars, sun, and solar disc) are favourites too. Modern motifs such as cars, rockets, locomotives, Mickey Mouse, boxers, footballers, etc, are also to be found, time and again, among the baking children do for Christmas. Figures with complex hair-styles are particularly old, and their unusual form — which scholars say points to an ancient sacrifice of hair — gains them the reputation of being particularly festive.

Many old forms have been preserved for the special festivals in the pre-Christmas period. The Martin's horn is baked for the 11th of November throughout the German Alps, in Swabia, Northern Thuringia, Silesia, Brandenburg, and Mecklenburg. The name and shape indicate that this was originally intended as a substitute for a horned animal due to be slaughtered. It was later reinterpreted as the herdsman's horn since animals are supposed to be safely in from pasture on November the 11th. A more recent interpretation though sees this as St. Martin's "horn of plenty" as the bringer of gifts. New interpretations of old forms have thus constantly arisen over the centuries.

Elsewhere in Germany there are figures of the Saint with his Bishop's staff. In Düsseldorf, Heidelberg, Ravensburg, and elsewhere, you still find the old Martin's pretzel. Its shape has been reinterpreted to symbolise friendship and Christian love.

There are also many specially-shaped breads and biscuits for the festival of St. Nicholas on December the 6th when the Saint leaves presents — as he has since the 16th century — in the shoes children have put out in front of their door or by the fire. These biscuits most frequently depict Nicholas himself or his attendant Ruprecht, who punishes naughty children with his rod. In fact these pastry figures look more like hobgoblins or demons than a Bishop. Sweetbread men are a part of this festival in the Rhineland and Westphalia, and are known by a variety of names. These are male figures with a clay pipe. They are also available from commercial bakeries today. Their popularity is demonstrated by the fact that between 14,000 and 15,000 are sold in Osnabrück year after year. That means that every other child aged between three and fourteen is presented with such a figure. If you also take into account the figures baked at home, then almost every child in Osnabrück must enjoy such a sweetbread man.

Father Christmas and the Three Kings are also frequently depicted in a diversity of ways reflecting the area involved. The tendency today is to make such biscuits ever more colourful and sugary.

It is not possible to give more than a general idea of the wealth of forms available over the Christmas period. These shapes are enormously popular among children because there are no limits to imagination in such baking. You can even make three-dimensional figures. The process of baking does alter these shapes considerably though so the pleasures of artistic creation have to take that into account.

Baking tins   The use of baking tins may mean renunciation of one's own creativity but the biscuits made accord more closely with existing models. The simplest household biscuits shapes today are mainly made of tin or plastic. A wide range is available for the usual animal figures, heavenly bodies, hearts, etc.

Among the more elaborate baking equipment, there are what are known as waffle irons, which are again enjoying increasing popularity. Making waffles for important festivals is an old custom which can be followed back to the 12th century. Dutch bakers were parti-

Colourful marzipan fruit and Christmas figures are an indispensable part of German baking.

cularly celebrated for this biscuit, and probably introduced it into Germany. In Saxony-Anhalt, the Brandenburg Marches, Lower Saxony, and, above all, in Westphalia, waffles or grid cakes have long been traditional at Christmas. In Westphalia, these grid cakes used to be baked on those heavy, old-fashioned irons, which have now been replaced in homes by modern electric irons.

Biscuit forms   Biscuit forms provide a very popular and a historically highly significant way of baking for Christmas. These used to be hollowed out with a carver's knife from the wood of a pear or cherry tree, and later from lime. The dough is pressed into these hollowed-out sections for such biscuits as the Springerle or the Spekulatius. The former was particularly popular in Nuremberg and in many other Franconian and Swabian towns in the 17th and 18th centuries, whilst the latter comes from the Lower Rhine area. Carving such forms was a full-time occupation which dated back to the 13th century and survived until around 1850. A few such carvers are still to be found in the Federal Republic today. Spekulatius biscuits are mainly manufactured by machine today but there are still firms that produce such forms. In earlier times, these wooden forms were embellished with religious and other scenes. During the Baroque age, forms were decorated with popular motifs such as horsemen, a leaping stag, a girl at a spinning wheel, fashionable ladies, an infant in swaddling clothes, hearts, and so on. Nuremberg patricians even had their family arms cut on such utensils. People from all levels of society used wooden forms for their Nuremberg gingerbread, and for aniseed and marzipan biscuits. These were minor works of art, and some of the old forms are still employed today.

Christmas loaves and fruit cakes   Christmas loaves constitute another very popular and widespread category of Christmas cheer. These cakes bear such regionally diverse names as Stollen, Striezel, Stuten, Früchtebrot, and Hutzelbrot. These cakes are long and wedge-shaped at the two ends. The most celebrated is perhaps the Stollen, a Bohemian-Saxon recipe, that was first mentioned in the year 1329. Scholars have sometimes said that the Stollen symbolises a boar, and at others the young Christ wrapped in swaddling clothes. The Saxon or Dresden Stollen are the most famous of all. The Electors of Saxony used to make presents of Stollen to their royal nephews all over the world, and even today the Stollen remains a very popular Christmas gift with Dresden almond and sultana Stollen despatched far and wide. Many regional and highly diverse variants of the Stollen are very well-known too. Apart from such Christmas loaves, there are also many fruit breads with the Swabian Hutzelbrot, made from dried pears, among the classics of German Christmas baking. These fruit breads follow on from what were

Christmas cookies — the Springerle still popular in Southern Germany today.

once fertility offerings. They also had the advantage of keeping throughout the winter so large amounts used to be baked in autumn as supplies for hard times. That also provided an opportunity for preserving the fruits of summer.

Spiced cakes   Spiced cakes are among the oldest, best-known, and most popular of Christmas consumables. These are usually thin honeyed biscuits. Honey was used instead of sugar for sweetening everywhere until about 400 years ago. The liberal use of spices of all kinds in this recipe is another characteristic mediaeval custom. Pepper was particularly rare and expensive at that time, a kind of status symbol, and almost became a synonym for spice. That may be why pepper is not used in many old recipes for these Pepper Cakes but was replaced by considerable quantities of cardamom and lemon peel, almonds and nutmeg, ginger, cloves, pimento, cinnamon, vanilla, and rose water. The origins of such spiced cakes are to be found in the kitchens of monasteries and castles, and a number of legends centre around the development of regional specialities. There is a story about a pious nun called Catharine at the Cistercian Nunnery at Thorn, who made a small elongated cake from flour, honey, and spices on her name day in the year 1312. This turned out well and she generously shared it out among the local populace who were so overjoyed by this unexpected and delicious gift that they called it a Catherine cake. The nun also gave the recipe to anyone who wished to have it. Since that time, Catherine cakes have been baked at Thorn and elsewhere on November the 25th. It is, however, more probable that the cake received its name from the fact that in earlier times its baking and sale were only permitted between St. Catherine's Day and Christmas.

In former times, these spiced cakes were mainly produced on a commercial basis. There was even a bakers guild which kept a strict watch over quality and sales. The most celebrated makers of spiced cakes were to be found in Nuremberg, the centre of the trade, and in Erlangen, Offenburg, Cologne, Basle, Breslau, Thorn, and Danzig.

Christmas fare for children also includes gingernuts, and the baking and assembling of a gingerbread house, which consists of a honey cake decorated with a multitude of colourful biscuits, sweets, and icing sugar. An old custom lays down that this gingerbread house can be slowly plundered and eaten up by children till Twelfth Night.

Many other Christmas biscuits are highly spicy too. On no other occasion is such a range of spices so lavishly employed as in this pre-Christmas baking. The outcome includes cinnamon stars,

A large 18th century baking mould embellished with the "Adoration of the Three Kings".

cinnamon pretzels, coriander strips, cardomon biscuits, saffron twist, ginger biscuits, aniseed loops, gingerbread, and a spiced layer cake, which includes honey, cinnamon, cardamom, cloves, aniseed, pimento, nutmeg blossoms, and vanilla.

Doughnuts, pancakes, etc. Cakes and pastries cooked in deep oil are eaten everywhere in the Federal Republic to mark New Year. These doughnuts and other cakes used to play a much greater part in the seasonal festivities. They are mainly eaten on New Year's Eve since they are intended as a symbol of affluence, a fat year. Almost everywhere used to have its own specialities with their particular names: Krapfen, Kroffel, Küchli, Mutzen, Schleifchen, Pfannkuchen, Hasenöhrchen, Raderkuchen, and so on. Berlin doughnuts are particularly popular, and there are large amounts of them on the festive table at New Year.

Marzipan There must be marzipan under every Christmas tree since this has been among the most delicate, decorative, and popular of goodies for centuries. Lübeck and Königsberg marzipan are the most celebrated of all, and are commercially produced in large amounts and sent to many countries. Both kinds are made from grated almonds, sugar, and rose water, and the Königsberg variety keeps for particularly long.

Christmas and baking have been extremely closely linked in Germany since time immemorial. A diversity and wealth of forms have been preserved over the centuries even though the more weighty cultural associations may have yielded today to more playful and aesthetic emphases.

Main dishes The former diversity of characteristic main dishes served at Christmas has not survived to such an extent as the confusing variety of seasonal cookies. The fact that Christmas has increasingly become a secular rather than a Christian festival has led to the disappearance of old, simple, and local dishes. Today the usual dishes for Sundays and special occasions predominate — particularly on Christmas Eve and Christmas Day.

A survey of traditional German meals at Christmas demonstrates the wide range of customary dishes and local variations. Certain features recur time and again though: pork, a gruel-like element, peas, beans, fish roe, and poppy seeds. The connection with fertility plays a great part in all these dishes. In some parts of Germany, there exists an express injunction that you should eat seven or nine dishes. Even though Christmas Eve was also a Church festival in earlier times, meat was never completely eliminated from the evening meal on this day.

Even today, the most usual meal on the 24th or the 25th of December is still roast pork with a variety of local trimmings. In towns though, roast goose is increasingly frequent — even though in previous centuries this was mainly a meal for St. Martin's Day,

An 18th century Aachen baking mould with "Christ Child".

a custom that can be traced back to the 13th century. In earlier times, St. Martin's Day was an important event in the farm economy. In many places this was the day for terminating or entering on new employment, and for handing over payment in kind, and was viewed as the end of the harvest season. The fact that the Martin's Day goose has become the Christmas goose mainly results from changes in organisation of the farming year, and from St. Martin's Day not being a public holiday any longer. There are still characteristic ways of preparing the goose even today, particularly with regard to the spices. East Prussians still use a lot of marjoram and stuff the goose with apples, people from Mecklenburg mainly employ thyme, and in Schleswig-Holstein the preference is for sweet spices, especially sugared raisins. Carp is another main dish at Christmas or New Year in Germany today, and there are local variations in the way it is cooked.

Gruel   Gruel used to be the dish with which the year was ended but has almost completely vanished now — except for a form made with peas. An old popular belief has it that you should eat peas at Christmas because baby Jesus lay on pea-straw. Cold meals — particularly sausages and potato salad — are frequent at New Year so as to relieve the house-wife of work.

Roast apples   Roast apples, a delight arousing many Christmas memories for the
and drinks   older generation, should not be forgotten either. The aroma of roast apples again pervades homes — as part of the general return to "Grandma's cooking" — and is once more an element in a centuries-old Christmas atmosphere.

Christmas drinks include the warm drinks characteristic of this cold time of year with a great deal of rum grog in North Germany and a variety of Christmas punches. Sparkling wine is drunk an New Year's Eve.

It is not possible here to provide more than a brief survey of the wealth of food and drink associated with the Christmas period. The following selection of recipes — more or less arbitrarily chosen — cannot lay any claim to completeness either. It may, however, lead readers to start baking or cooking, and thus help to capture something of Christmas.

Drinking is a part of the Christmas feast — here a "Schnelle" (stone-jar) with crib scene from Siegburg in the Rhineland.

Gingerbread witch's house, decorated with sweets, biscuits, and a lot of icing sugar.

XIV.

Recipes

500 gr. golden syrup, 200 gr. sugar, 12 gr. cinnamon, 15 gr. aniseed, 9 gr. clove powder, a pinch of cardamom, 7 gr. bicarbonate of soda, dissolved in a little water, 750 gr. flour, some milk, and coarse granulated sugar.

Aachener Printen (Aachen Nut Biscuits)

Bring the sugar and syrup to the boil. Add the spices. Then take off the stove. When lukewarm, mix in the flour. Add the dissolved bicarbonate of soda. Knead the dough thoroughly once again, and leave to stand overnight. Roll out so that the dough is half a centimetre thick. Cut into strips about 2 cm wide and 10 cm long. Place in a greased tin, brush with milk, sprinkle with sugar, and bake in a pre-heated oven.

Heat: 190 °C. Baking time: around 15 minutes.

4 eggs, 250 gr. sugar, 250—300 gr. flour, 1 tbsp. aniseed (preferably 'double purified').

Anisplätzchen (Aniseed Biscuits)

Beat the eggs and sugar until they are very frothy — for at least half an hour if by hand. Then add the aniseed and the flour (slightly warmed). Grease a tray and sprinkle with flour. Then either roll out the dough and cut out little round biscuits, or cover the tray with little heaps of dough (2 tsp. each). Leave this out overnight at room temperature, and then bake until the biscuits are light-brown.

Heat: 160 °C. Time: around 25 minutes.

500 gr. flour, 30 gr. yeast, ¼ l. luke-warm milk, 50 gr. sugar, a pinch of salt, grated peel of one lemon, jam for the filling, cooking oil, and c. 100 gr. sugar for sprinkling on afterwards.

Berliner Pfannkuchen (Doughnuts)

Mix the ingredients, beating well and letting rise. Then roll out the dough (1 cm thick) on a floured baking tray. Use a wine glass to mark out circles on half of this dough. Put some jam in the middle of each of these circles, brush the edges of the circles with egg-white, and cover with the other half of the dough. Cut out the doughnuts, press the edges together, and let them rise again. Then carefully put the doughnuts (upside down) into the oil (just below boiling). Put a top on the pot for the first 5 minutes so that the doughnuts swell up. Then turn the doughnuts and cook for a further 5 minutes. Put the finished doughnuts on a grid so that the fat can drip off, and sprinkle with sugar while they are still hot.

Dresdner Christstollen (Dresden Christmas Stollen)

500 gr. raisins, 125 gr. currants, 100 gr. candied lemon peel, 100 gr. candied orange peel, 250 gr. almonds, 2 liqueur glasses of rum, 1 kg flour, 120 gr. yeast, 350 gr. sugar, 1/4 l. milk, 375 gr. butter, 125 gr. butter for brushing on afterwards, 100 gr. icing sugar.

Pour the rum over the raisins, currants, finely chopped candied peel, and the peeled and chopped almonds. Stand overnight — covered. Crumble the yeast, and mix with the luke-warm milk. Add to the flour together with the soft butter and sugar, and knead into a smooth dough. Cover and leave to rise in a warm place for 20 minutes. Add the fruit that has been steeped in the rum. Knead thoroughly once again, and let the dough (covered) rise for another 30 minutes. Knead once more. Roll out on a surface covered with a little flour to make an oval slab about 3 cm. thick. Make a groove with a large rolling pin along the length of the centre of the dough, and then fold one half over the other. Let the Stollen rise for another 15 minutes on a greased baking tray. Bake for 20 minutes in an oven pre-heated to 200° — and then for 70 Minutes at 175°. If the Stollen gets too brown, cover with some greaseproof paper. Immediately after baking, brush the Stollen with melted butter and sprinkle thickly with icing sugar.

Früchtebrot (Fruit bread)

3 eggs, 120 gr. icing sugar, 1 packet vanilla sugar (c. 30 gr.), 1/2 tsp. cinnamon, a pinch of clove powder, grated peel of half an orange, 50 gr. finely chopped almonds, 125 gr. chopped hazel nuts, 125 gr. diced figs, 200 gr. raisins, 125 gr. chopped candied lemon peel, 50 gr. cornflour, 1 tsp. baking powder.

Beat the eggs, vanilla and icing sugar until the mixture is very frothy, adding the spices and other ingredients in succession. Last of all add the baking powder mixed with the cornflour. Put the dough into a cake-tin lined with greaseproof paper, and bake in a pre-heated oven. Do not cut this fruit bread until it is completely cold.

Heat: 200°C. Time: around 70 minutes.

12 cooking apples, 24 sugar cubes, 50 gr. sliced almond, 50 gr. raisins, 12 tsp. raspberry jam, 2 tbsp. rum, 50 gr. butter.

Wash and dry the apples, and take out the cores. Push a cube of sugar into each of the apples from underneath. Mix the almonds, raisins, and raspberry jam with the rum. Fill the apples with this mixture and top with the rest of the sugar cubes. Put the apples in a low pudding dish greased with 10 gr. of butter — plus a dab of butter on top of each apple. Bake for 45 minutes in a pre-heated oven (200°C.).

Großmutters
Bratäpfel
(Grandmother's
roast apples)

250 gr. almonds, 250 gr. icing sugar, 1 egg-white, 1 tbsp. rose water.

Dry the shelled almonds well, and put through the grinder twice. Mix with the egg-white and rose water to form a smooth paste. Leave to stand overnight. Form little pretzels, rolls, and loaves out of this bulk marzipan. Brush these with egg-yolk, and put on a baking tray covered with greaseproof paper. Roast fast with the oven set to a high temperature so that the marzipan quickly turns brown.

Königsberger
Marzipan
(Königsberg
marzipan)

500 gr. flour, 40 gr. yeast, 1/8 l. milk, 80 gr. butter, 80 gr. sugar, 1 egg, the grated peel of a lemon, 2 tbsp. melted butter, 1 egg yolk, sliced almonds. Filling: 125 gr. sultanas and 125 gr. currants mixed with 80 gr. grated almonds or nuts and 125 gr. sugar. For the icing: 150 gr. icing sugar mixed with 3 to 4 tbsp. hot water.

Prepare a dough from these ingredients. When this has risen, divide into 10 to 15 parts. Roll each of these out into a rectangle about 1 1/2 cm. long. Brush this with butter, put in the filling, and roll together. Form this roll into a crescent shape, brush with egg yolk, sprinkle with sliced almonds, and let this rise again. Bake on a greased tray in a pre-heated oven, and then add the icing whilst still hot.

Heat: 200°C. Time: around 25 minutes.

Martinihörner
(Martin's horns)

Nürnberger Pfefferkuchen (Nuremberg spiced cakes)

280 gr. icing sugar, 4 eggs (separated), 1 tsp. cinnamon, a pinch of clove powder, a pinch of white pepper, the juice and grated peel of half an orange, the grated peel of half a lemon, 140 gr. of ground almonds, 140 gr. of peeled and chopped almonds, 140 gr. of chopped candied lemon, 70 gr. wheat flour, 70 gr. cornflour. Peeled and halved almonds for decoration. Icing: 50 gr. icing sugar mixed with some orange juice.

Mix the icing sugar and the egg yolk until this is very frothy. Then add the spices, orange and lemon peel, almonds, and candied lemon. Finally add the flour, cornflour, and egg-white (beaten until stiff) at the same time. Cut out finger-thick round shapes, decorate with half almonds, and bake slowly. Ice with the orange juice mixture whilst the cakes are still warm.

Heat: 170°C. Time: around 25 minutes.

Pfeffernüsse (Ginger nuts)

500 gr. flour, 3 level tsp. baking powder, 300 gr. sugar, 2 eggs, 6 tbsp. milk, a pinch of ginger, cloves, nutmeg, and white pepper, 1 tsp. cinnamon, the grated peel of half a lemon and half an orange, 60 gr. grated almonds, 30 gr. candied lemon diced very small. Icing: 200 gr. icing sugar with 2 to 3 tbsp. hot water mixed in until this is syrupy in consistency.

Mix the flour and baking powder, and sieve onto a board. Make a hollow in the middle. Add the eggs, sugar, milk, and spices, and work in part of the flour. Distribute the rest of the ingredients throughout this mixture, and knead a smooth dough. Roll out 1 cm thick, and cut out discs between 2 and 3 cm in diameter. Put on a greased tray, and bake in a pre-heated oven. Ice when cold.

Heat: 175°C. Time: around 20 minutes.

Rheinische Mutzemandeln (Rhenish almonds)

50 gr. butter, 125 gr. sugar, 2 eggs, 375 gr. flour mixed with 1 packet baking powder, 2 tbsp. rum. Lard or oil for deep frying. Castor sugar for coating.

Whip the butter, sugar, and eggs. Add the rum and then the mixture of flour and baking powder. Leave the dough standing for half an hour in a cold place. Then roll out very thin, and cut out small almond-shaped biscuits. Cook in boiling fat. Let the fat drip off and roll in sugar.

150 gr. roast veal, 80 gr. salami, 1 filleted herring, 250 gr. soft apples, 500 gr. potatoes, 2 pickled gherkins, mayonnaise, ½ cup milk, ½ cup meat broth, 10 walnuts, 10 hazel nuts, 2 eggs, parsley, and optionally 1 beetroot.

Rheinischer Weihnachtssalat (Rhenish Christmas salad)

Cut all the ingredients into small strips or cubes. Add pepper, salt, mayonnaise, and liquid, and mix well. Chop the nuts, parsley, and hard-boiled eggs, and sprinkle over the salad.

500 gr. flour, 40 gr. yeast, ¼ l. milk, 100 gr. butter, 80 gr. sugar, ½ tsp. salt, 1 egg. Filling: 250 gr. scalded and ground poppy seeds, 150 gr. sugar, 50 gr. currants, 50 gr. sultanas, 50 gr. grated almonds, the grated peel of half a lemon, a pinch of cinnamon, and 3 to 4 tbsp. milk. 50 gr. melted butter. For icing: 150 gr. icing sugar (to be mixed with 3 to 4 tbsp. hot water).

Schlesischer Mohnstollen (Silesian poppy-seed Stollen)

Make a semi-firm dough from the ingredients, and after this has risen roll it out into a rectangular shape, finger-thick. Sprinkle melted butter over this, and spread out the filling up to 2 cm. from the edges. Roll the Stollen together, put on a greased tray, and let rise once again. Brush this with melted butter, and bake in a pre-heated oven. Ice the Stollen when still hot.

Heat: 200 °C. Time: around 45 minutes.

1 to 1½ kg. carp, 125 to 200 gr. of both raisins and almonds, 100 gr. gingerbread for the sauce, 1 tbsp. flour, 1 to 2 onions, 2 carrots, 1 stick of cellery, 2 cloves, 1 bay leaf, 40—50 gr. butter, 1 to 2 tbsp. sugar, 2 tbsp. vinegar, 1 l. dark beer.

Schlesischer Weihnachts-karpfen (Silesian Christmas carp)

Scale, gut, and wash the fish carefully. Bring the head, tail, vegetables, cloves, bay leaf, and beer to the boil. Skim off, and boil for a further 30 minutes. Slightly brown the flour in the butter, and add the sugar. Mix in the strained fish stock, grated gingerbread, raisins, and chopped almonds, and cook for 10 minutes. Cut the carp into pieces, and simmer in the creamy sauce until ready. The blood of fresh carp can be mixed with vinegar and added to the sauce. Eat with boiled potatoes or dumplings.

Thorner Katharinchen (Thorn Catharine cakes)

250 gr. honey, 50 gr. sugar, 50 gr. butter, 1/2 tsp. cinnamon, a pinch of clove powder and ginger, 1 egg yolk, 250 gr. wheat flour, 100 gr. cornflour, 1 tsp. creamed tartar.

Heat up the honey, sugar, and butter to boiling point, and then take off the stove. Add the spices, and leave to cool. Next add the egg yolk, flour, and dissolved creamed tartar, and knead the dough thoroughly. Leave standing — covered in a warm place — for an hour. Roll out 3 mm. thick, cut into small elongated shapes, and spread these out on a greased, floured tray so that they do not touch one another. Brush with luke-warm water, and bake in a pre-heated oven.

Heat: 200 °C. Time: around 20 minutes.

Zimtsterne (Cinnamon stars)

4 egg whites, 250 gr. castor sugar, 5 gr. cinnamon, 300 gr. unpeeled grated almonds, and some icing sugar.

Whip the egg whites and sugar for 20 to 30 minutes. Set aside about 3 tbsp. of this quantity. Add the cinnamon and grated almonds to what remains, and roll out this paste on the icing sugar to a thickness of around 5 mm. Cut out the stars and lay on a greased baking tray. Brush these stars with the whipped mixture put aside for this purpose, and put in the pre-heated oven.

Heat: 170 °C. Time: 20 to 25 minutes.

XV.

Bibliography

Alle Jahre wieder . . . A collection of Christmas stories, poems, letters, and songs. Collected by E. F. Karrer. Stuttgart 1964.

Das Andernacher Gesangbuch (Cologne 1608). Facsimile. Edited — with concluding remarks — by Michael Härting. In Denkmäler Rheinischer Musik, published by the Arbeitsgemeinschaft für Rheinische Musikgeschichte. Vol. 18. Düsseldorf 1970.

Angermann, Gertrud: Das Martinsbrauchtum in Bielefeld und Umgebung im Wandel der Zeiten. In: Rheinisch-Westfälische Zeitschrift für Volkskunde, edited by Karl Meisen and Bruno Schier. Vol. IV, 1957. Pp 231—256.

Das Atlantis Weihnachtsbuch. Edited by Claus & Liselotte Hansmann and Roswitha Schlötterer. Zurich 1977.

Brautlacht, Claire (Ed.): Stille Nacht. Christmas stories. Kevelaer 1959.

Cassels, Paulus. Weihnachten — Ursprung, Bräuche und Aberglauben. Berlin. Reprinting of the 1862 edition — Sändig, Walluf near Wiesbaden. 1973.

Cordes, Alexandra (Ed.): Die schönsten Weihnachtsgeschichten der Welt. Munich 1977.

Engelmeier, Paul: Westfälische Weihnachtskrippen aus dem 18. und 19. Jahrhundert. In: Festschrift für Joseph Klersch. Published by the Heimatverein Alt-Köln. Cologne—Neuss 1963. Pp 27—36.

Geppert, Waldtraut-Ingeborg: Das Kirchenlied. In: Reallexikon der Deutschen Literaturgeschichte. Estab. by P. Merker and W. Stammler. 2nd edition, edited by W. Kohlschmidt and W. Mohr. Vol. I. Berlin 1958. Pp. 819—852.

Hauschildt, Karl: Die Christusverkündigung im Weihnachtslied unserer Kirchen. Göttingen 1952.

Hein, Nikolaus: Das Buch vom Sankt Martin. Zurich 1962.

Hoffmann-Herreros, Johann (Ed.): Weihnachtsgeschichten. Topos paperback vol. 42. Mainz 1975.

Hole, Christina: Christmas and its customs. New York 1958.

Hoyer, Franz A.: Dreikönigsbuch. Stories and poems about the Three Wise Men. Düsseldorf 1949.

Kissling, Hermann: Das Weihnachtsbild. A mediaeval cycle of pictures. Ratingen/Kastellaun 1972.

Koren, Hanns: Volksbrauch im Kirchenjahr. Salzburg/Leipzig 1934.

Krogmann, Willy: Die Wurzeln des Weihnachtsbaumes. In: Rheinisches Jahrbuch für Volkskunde. Ed. Karl Meisen. Vols. 13 & 14. Bonn 1963. Pp 60—80.

Lauffer, Otto: Der Weihnachtsbaum in Glaube und Brauch. Berlin and Leipzig 1934.

Lebold, Reinhold: Die Entwicklung der Bescherungsspiele und die nordostfränkischen Einkehrspiele am Weihnachtsabend. Würzburg 1971.

Lenotre, G.: Contes Historiques de Noël (dtv two-language version). Munich 1973.

Meisen, Karl: Die Heiligen Drei Könige und ihr Festtag im volkskundlichen Glauben und Brauch. Cologne 1949.

Metken, Sigrid: Sankt Nikolaus in Kunst und Volksbrauch. Duisburg 1966.

Morgen Kinder wirds was geben. A Saxon Christmas book edited by Helmut Sieber. Frankfurt am Main 1966.

Poston, Elizabeth: The Penguin Book of Christmas Carols. Middlesex 1965.

Ratzenböck, Anneliese: Der Christbaum — Geschichten und Geschichte. Linz (Austria) 1985.

Riemann, Erhard: Der Schimmelreiter und sein vermummtes Ge-
folge. In: Erfreue dich Himmel, erfreue dich Erde. Christmas poems
and stories, songs and customs. Published by Landsmannschaft Ostpreußen 1973.

Riemann, Erhard: Die Sternsinger. In: Erfreue dich Himmel, erfreue
dich Erde. Christmas poems and stories, songs and customs.
Published by Landsmannschaft Ostpreußen 1973.

Riemerschmidt, Ulrich: Weihnachten – Kult und Brauch – einst und
jetzt, Hamburg 1962.

Rietschel, Georg: Weihnachten in Kirche, Kunst und Volksleben
(Sammlung Illustrierter Monographien Vol. V). Bielefeld and Leipzig 1902.

Ruland, Josef: Die volkstümliche Verehrung der Heiligen Drei
Könige und das sich daraus entwickelnde Brauchtum. In: — und
sie folgten seinem Stern. The Book of the Three Holy Kings. Ed.
Adam Wienand. Cologne 1964.

Sauermann, Dietmar: Westfälische Martinslieder nach den Samm-
lungen des Atlas der deutschen Volkskunde. In: Rheinisch-Westfälische Zeitschrift für Volkskunde. Ed. Karl Meisen and Bruno
Schier. Vol. 16, 1969. Pp 70—104.

Sauermann, Dietmar (ed.): Weihnachten in Westfalen um 1900.
Münster 1976.

Schlißke, Otto: Apfel, Nuß und Mandelkern. 2nd edition. Glad-
beck 1977.

Stille Nacht, Heilige Nacht. The history of a song. Ed. Alois
Schmaus and Lenz Kris-Rettenbeck. 2nd edition. Innsbruck-Munich
1968.

Tille, Alexander: Die Geschichte der deutschen Weihnacht. Leipzig
no date (1893).

Unvergängliche Weihnacht. Texts assembled by Erich F. Karrer.
Stuttgart 1964.

Vossen, Carl: Sankt Martin. Sein Leben und Fortwirken in Gesin-
nung, Brauchtum und Kunst. Düsseldorf 1975.

Vossen, Rüdiger: Weihnachtsbräuche in aller Welt, Hamburgisches
Museum für Völkerkunde, Hamburg 1985.

Weber-Kellermann, Ingeborg: Das Weihnachtsfest – Eine Kultur- und Sozialgeschichte der Weihnachtszeit, Munich and Lucerne 1987.

Weihnacht. In: Trübners Deutsches Wörterbuch, estab. by Alfred Götze and ed. by Walther Mitzka. Vol. VIII, Berlin 1956. Pp 87—89.

Weihnacht der Welt. Ed. Konrad Federer. Zürich 1956.
Das große Weihnachtsbuch. Published by the Südwest Verlag, Munich 1976. Songs — games — stories — things to make — poems — recipes.

Die Weihnachtskrippe. Published since about 1926 on behalf of the Landesgemeinschaft der Krippenfreunde in Rheinland und Westfalen. 41 yearbooks. Telgte/Westphalia, no date.

Weiser, Lily: Jul — Weihnachtsgeschenke und Weihnachtsbaum. Stuttgart/Gotha 1923.

Wiemer, Rudolf Otto (Ed.): Wo wir Menschen sind. A collection of new Christmas stories. Düsseldorf 1974.

Zender, Matthias: Räume und Schichten mittelalterlicher Heiligenverehrung in ihrer Bedeutung für die Volkskunde. Düsseldorf 1959.

Zenetti, Lothar: Das allerschönste Fest. Ein Frankfurter Weihnachtsbuch. Frankfurt am Main 1977.

XVI.

Illustrations

The author and publisher would like to thank the following museums and other sources of pictures for their assistance:

Amt für Rheinische Landeskunde, Ausstellung Museum Burg Frankenberg in Aachen (p. 133)

Archiv und Museum der Stadt Hallein (Österreich) (p. 77—79)

Artemis, Zürich (p. 37, 41, 93, 129)

Bildarchiv Preußischer Kulturbesitz (p. 61)

Franz Burda GmbH, Offenburg (p. 57)

Diözesanmuseum, Rottenburg (p. 149)

Dombauverwaltung Köln (45, 151)

Fichtelgebirgsmuseum in Wunsiedel (p. 63, 95)

Gruner + Jahr, Hamburg (p. 55)

Henssel Verlag, Berlin (p. 51)

Historisches Museum in Frankfurt am Main (p. 27, 39)

Jahreszeiten-Verlag, Hamburg (p. 71)

Liebfrauenkirche Oberwesel (p. 9)

Wolf Lücking, München (p. 22, 39)

Museum für Niederrheinische Volkskunde Kevelaer (p. 17)

Österreichische Post- und Telegraphenverwaltung, Wien (p. 30)

Sammlung Maud Pohlmeyer (p. 55, 69)

Stadt Frankfurt am Main (p. 85)

Stadt München (p. 121)

Stadt Nürnberg (p. 34)

Stadt Siegburg (p. 135)

Weber, Heiner, in Seiffen (p. 91, 121)

Stadt Wermelskirchen (p. 69)

Städelsches Kunstinstitut in Frankfurt am Main (p. 91)

Time-Life-International (p. 127, 136)

Christmas Calendar

"Martin's gift of his cloak" — painting by a Swabian master around 1440.

November the 10th   St. Martin's Eve

"St. Martin, St. Martin, St. Martin is a good man . . ." — sing children every Martin's Eve. With this festivity, Christmas gets under way with its light, warmth, and many presents for children and adults amid the days and nights of winter.

November the 11th   St. Martin's Day

Who does not know the Advent wreath, made out of the greenery of fir embellished with four red or yellow candles? The children know all about it at any rate since when the first candle is lit on "Green Sunday" — the Sunday after November the 26th — the distribution of Christmas presents is less than four weeks away. In between there are three other Sundays in Advent and they are called: "Copper Sunday", "Silver Sunday" and "Golden Sunday".

November

10 11 12 13 14 15 16 17 18 19 20 21 22 23 24
25 26 27 28 29 30

"St. Nicholas" — the master of Schöppingen (Westphalia) around 1443.

"Adoration of the Child" — The m

December the 4th   St. Barbara's Day
December the 5th   St. Nicholas' Eve
"Nicholas, come into our house/Start to unpack your sack!" The Christmas spirit spreads among children as St. Nicholas and his attendant Ruprecht go from house to house, generously distributing his "gifts" as from time immemorial.
December the 6th   St. Nicholas' Day

December the 13th   St. Lucia's Day
December the 21th   St. Thomas's Day
December the 22nd   The start of Winter
December the 24th   Christ's Eve
(Start of the Twelve Nights of Christmas)
December the 25th   Christmas Day
(Birth of Christ) "For unto us a child is born . . ." The silent, holy nigh

De

nöppingen (Westphalia) around 1445.

"St. Sylvester" — painting from the Rhineland around 1420.

as come — and this song, dedicated all children as well as to the Christ hild, is to be heard in every church. hristmas, so long looked forward to, as at last arrived. Everyone, whether hristian or not, endeavours to meet s fellows with friendship.

ecember the 26th   Second Day of hristmas (St. Stephen's Day)

December the 28th   Feast of the Innocents (Massacre of children at Bethlehem)
December the 31st   St. Sylvester's Eve
Excitement errupts all over Germany as midnight approaches on New Years Eve with the old year taking its leave and the new starting. Brilliant rockets shoot into the heavens, "thunderclaps" explode, and champagne corks pop.

"Adoration of the Three Kings" — Konrad von Soest, Wildung altar, 1403.

January the 1st   New Year's Day
January the 5th   End of the Twelve Nights of Christmas
January the 6th   Feast of the Three Kings (Epiphany)
"O come let us adore him": the birth of Our Lord is marked by particular splendour during the Feast of Epiphany. Like the Three Wise Men, the faithful go to church to celebrate this manifestation.
February the 2nd   Purification of the Virgin Mary

January/February

1 2 3 4 5 6 7 8 9 10 11 12 13 14 15
16 17 18 19 20 21 22 23 24 25 26 27 28 29 30
31   1 2